Matthias Lederer
Dieter Raake
Matthias Kurz

# The BSC Cookbook

Vol. 1 – Ingredients for a Successful Balanced Scorecard

Institute of Innovative Process Management

ISBN: 978-3-945577-00-4

# Abstract

The Balanced Scorecard (BSC) by Kaplan and Norton is considered to be one of the most successful and widely used management concepts today. It constitutes an instrument for the strategic management of organizational and process performance.

Yet this concept has a fundamental gap: There are no general rules that outline the principles for the successful implementation and execution of a BSC. Typically, only isolated recommendations and single success factors have been researched that state the results from individual cases, and expert opinions or investigations in a specific field. This book introduces a cooking recipe for successfully implementing a process-oriented BSC within a company. This recipe is based on the insights gained during a real-word project conducted at a large engineering company.

The book starts with introducing the BSC implementation project along with the surrounding setting at the company. After a brief introduction to the original BSC approach proposed by Kaplan and Norton, the cooking recipes are introduced in an easy-to-understand format. Each ingredient is illustrated by an example from the above-mentioned real-world project. For assisting the reader in conducting similar BSC implementation projects, the appendix contains helpful and tested templates.

# Foreword

In management science and practice, the *Balanced Scorecard* is a well-established management method for developing and implementing strategies.

Despite the tremendous success of the Balanced Score card, enterprises are still struggling with applying the balanced scorecard in a way that ensures lasting results. Although the method explicitly emphasizes that strategies should consider several dimensions, many strategy development and implementation projects tend to limit the application of the Balanced Score Card to the financial dimension.

While such a one-sided strategic focus can often yield short-term cost optimizations, there are many examples of enterprises which lost their capability to reinvent themselves in order to respond changing market forces after conducting a series of cost-cutting programs.

These examples inspired the ongoing *Business Process Transparency Management* (BPTM) research project at the Friedrich-Alexander-University which has the mission to align business processes and strategies in a holistic way which covers *all* dimensions of the balanced score card. Specifically, the project develops methods to devise, implement, and measure such holistic strategies.

In order to test the methods, concepts, and tools developed by the project, they are applied in multiple real-world strategy development and/or implementation projects conducted at several large European companies.

This book presents one of the core methods developed in the BPTM project which provides a clear and concise "recipe" for (i) reengineering business processes in a strategy-oriented way and (2) measuring the performance of these reengineered processes. As this "recipe" has been successfully applied in a large European engineering company, it provides valuable lessons learned for similar projects. In order to facilitate such projects, extensive examples explain the "ingredients" of said "recipe" while detailed downloadable templates for Microsoft Word and Excel help in getting up to speed.

The engineering company which we conducted the example project in requested us not to share the name or too much specifics of the company in order to ensure that competitors cannot use the information provided in this book. Therefore, we are not able to explicitly mention all those who contributed too the project. Still, we would very much like to thank them for their invaluable input to the project.

While this book focuses on well-established concepts and methods, the second volume will introduce and discuss newer – but less tested – developments and trends of the Balanced Score Card. These new and exciting spices from the second volume are intended to complement the more traditional recipe provided in this book.

As the BPTM project is steadily progressing, more information and research results will be published. We would like to invite the reader to learn more about the BPTM effort on the project website www.process-transparency.com.

Nuremberg, in July 2014     Matthias Lederer
                            Dieter Raake
                            Matthias Kurz


                   bsc-cookbook@process-transparency.com

# Contents

# 1    Introduction

The subtitle **Translating Strategy into Action** of Kaplan and Norton's book **The Balanced Scorecard** states the gist of the most successful concept for modern performance measurement and management in our days: Strategies are of little value if there is no plan how to make them actionable and implement them in the operations of enterprises.

The Balanced Score Card (BSC) approach introduced by Kaplan and Norton shows practitioners how to link an enterprise's vision, its strategy, and its operative business. The large number of successful case studies[1] demonstrates the practicability of the approach. Today, the Balanced Scorecard (BSC) is used in an estimated half of large-sized enterprises worldwide (Rigby 2003). When applying the BSC successfully, enterprises can benefit from optimized internal communication, effective alignment of business operations, and ultimately higher revenues (Letza 1996, pp. 54ff.; Niven 2002; Kaplan and Norton 2001).

## 1.1    Objectives and Target Audience

However, realizing these BSC's potentials requires substantial preparation and careful consideration of the BSC success factors. This is a challenging task for many managers who have little experience with BSC projects, as literature from research and practice proposes a vast number of potentially contradicting success factors. In an extensive search for success factors and barriers to implementation of

---

[1]    Refer e. g. to the studies and reports by Broccardo (2010, p. 90), Varma and Deshmukh (2009, pp. 12f.), Sim and Koh (2001, pp. 18ff.), Frigo and Krumwiede (1999, p. 45), and Umbeck, Lederer and Nitze (2009, pp. 383ff.).

the BSC, Matlachowsky (2008, p. 94) reaches the conclusion that currently no comprehensive and generally valid documentation of success principles for BSCs is available.

In order to address this issue, the authors analyzed a large body of research papers and case studies. Based on this meta analysis, it was possible to construct a consistent approach for the implementation within a company. In order to be certain that this framework is feasible a BSC implementation project at a large European plant construction company was conducted. Furthermore, the project was used to fine-tune the approach accordingly.

This book presents an easy-to-understand and easy-to-follow approach for implementing the BSC which is described using a cookbook metaphor. The book's indented target audience is managers who possess a working knowledge of management methods but who are not experts in BSC projects.

## 1.2   How to Read this Book

With this book's objective being an easy-to-understand introduction to successful BSC projects, the book's structure is intentionally pragmatic. Chapter 2 presents a BSC implementation project in a large European plant construction enterprise in the chemical industry, which based on this book's BSC recipes. This project is used for illustrating the BSC recipes throughout this book.

Chapter 3 explains the basic principles and concepts of the BSC. Based on this foundation, Chapter 4 introduces six ingredients that are vital for successful BSC implementations. Each ingredient represents a major aspect of a BSC implementation and is explained in a uniform way:

First, the ingredient is briefly *defined*. Then the *background* and related concepts of the ingredient are introduced. Readers may skip this background information and jump directly to the key *components* of each ingredient. After discussing the *benefits* and *restrictions* of the ingredient, the book suggests hints for *implement-*

*ing* the respective ingredient. An *example* shows how the ingredient has been used in the example project.

In appendix A, commonly used document templates for BSC projects are introduced. For the reader's convenience, these templates are available from the book's website (www.process-transparency.com) using the password *cooking*.

# 2 Example Scenario

All described ingredient base on a systematic literature analysis (see appendix B) taking 30 different best practices, scientific studies as well as manager reports and case studies into consideration. However, all presented parts of this cookbook also come from experiences the authors made in comprehensive applications of the BSC approach within large-sized companies. Due to confidentiality reasons, the name of the company cannot be named and details of the presented example project needed to be changed.

The actual design and implementation of a BSC cannot happen without knowledge of the organizational framework of a company. The need to examine the current strategy and existing management information systems follows directly from the BSC approach: All contents of the BSC are dependent on the vision and strategic objectives of an organization. This chapter will therefore briefly outline the given example scenario on which the ingredients for a successful scorecard are deducted from.

The BSC was developed on an overall corporate level because this was an actual requirement of the Management Board in charge. Furthermore the completed scorecard was then step by step cascaded to single processes and some departments such as logistics. In order to present actionable and comprehensible examples for all cookbook ingredient, the case of the logistic process as part of the SCM processes will be presented.

This sample scenario follows the idea of a process-oriented implementation within a clearly process-centric organizational structure. If the reader is faced with a more hierarchical and a low process-orientation within his or her organization, he or she can apply all guidelines and descriptions of this book by changing the process level into a department focus.

## 2.1 Basic Company Information

The ABC Plant Engineering[2] was founded in 1975 as a result of the merger of two large-sized corporations. It is headquartered in Vienna (Austria) and has several locations all around the world. ABC delivers and installs chemical industry as well as oil-based power plants and equipment for a wide range of technical applications.

The company's product and service portfolio covers the following areas:

- **Energy technology**: Energy technology is the business group that designs and builds power plants for sophisticated applications in the field of fossil energy production based on different types of oil.
- **Building**: This business group comprises all activities associated with planning and achievement of chemical industry buildings, their technical equipment and its maintenance.
- **Industry**: Conducted within this division is the planning of facilities and workflow systems for different areas. Examples are pharmaceuticals and fine chemicals.
- **Facility management**: Within this group all maintenance and support activities are pooled which are usually not the primary businesses of the building owners. Examples include engineering, maintenance, refurbishment, disposal, cleaning, postal services and inventory management.

So far nearly all the firm's activities were carried out as projects. This project-orientation stems from a long tradition in the two former companies. Although many projects include almost identical sequences, these were often handled as projects.

In the year of the BSC implementation project, the company achieved revenues of about one million euros and gained an order book of approximately 4 billion euros. ABC currently achieves 40% of its sales abroad.

---

2     The Company name was freely invented for this book.

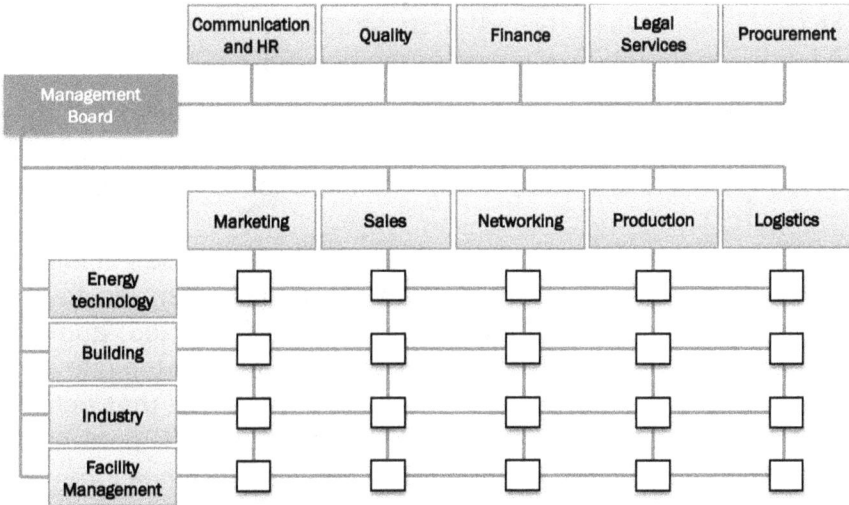

Figure 1: Organizational chart of ABC
[Source: own illustration]

## 2.2   Success of the Former BSC Efforts

Within ABC, the last BSC was in place until 2007 and currently no BSC is in use neither on corporate level nor on the levels of single processes or departments. However, a BSC was introduced around 1990. Since then the BSC has grown over time, has been adopted by various departments and was optimized by extensive internal training programs.

At the last documented stage of the former BSC, it was organized in the central quality department on behalf of the management board: Each quarter, one person in charge in the quality department asked different departments to provide the necessary actions for the corporate BSC via e-mail. Within the quality department, these sources were then compiled and summarized. The resulting BSC was added to the quarterly business reports of the management board. With the departure of this local hero within this department, the BSC was no longer supported and all other department stopped supplying data.

From the analysis of the historical situation, the following lessons can be drawn for the application of the new BSC:

- The former BSC was characterized by very detailed documentation and particularly good formal organization (e. g. definition of data sources, forms, visualization and description of figures).
  *These aspects should be maintained for a new BSC solution.*
- The processing of data delivery via e-mail often led to problems, because the data needed to be reformatted, and often the available data from the departments arrived too late.
  *Therefore a different technical implementation that achieves higher binding and has fewer interfaces has to be preferred.*
- The corporate BSC included only very general measures (e. g. sales and turnover, customer satisfaction, number of new projects). The interpretation possibilities were thus limited and the strategy reference was not always given since the old BSC was only presented as an appendix to management board reports.
  *The new BSC should therefore be really customized to the organization of ABC (e. g. tailored perspectives and strategy-driven measures).*
- The former BSC was organized only at the corporate level. Due to the lack of actual cascading in all departments, some participants thought that the BSC was only realizing an additional reporting system.
  *The new BSC should therefore be fully cascaded so that the concept comes to life. Furthermore, new indicators must be developed based on the strategy to overcome the pitfall of creating additional short-term reporting of already available data.*
- According to the statements of various employees, the involved participants of the former BSC could not recognize its actual added value.
  *It is important for a new BSC solution that all concerned departments and employees can see the benefits of this strategy-driven approach. It will be necessary to highlight that the BSC is a management tool (e. g. for strategy communication,*

*leading and coordinating employees, measuring strategy achievement and long-term analysis) instead of a short-term measurement system.*

## 2.3   Existing Performance Management System

No real BSC exist within ABC. However, two findings were discovered during the business analysis: First, many departments and process owners have a considerable interest in the implementation of a BSC (e. g. as a basis for ISO certification, as a reliable basis for target agreements for employees, to align actions with strategy, etc.). Second, in some departments and business process teams efforts were already made to implement frameworks which are comparable to the BSC (e. g. in the purchasing and HR processes).

The following aspects can summary the existing performance management system:

- **No uniform reporting**: The format, quality and quantity of re- porting is different in each department, business group and reporting line. Reporting is neither uniform nor aligned to cen- trally described rules. This frequently makes interpreting the results (e. g. across business groups) quite difficult.
- **Subsequent adjustment of strategy**: Often reports form pro- cess owners and head of departments are subsequently adapted to the strategy of ABC, rather than using the strategy as starting point for selecting and interpreting indicators. Some departments clearly use local strategies for their report- ing documents, but often these are not openly communicated within ABC. A consistent target system is missing.
- **Good design and documentation**: The layout of the reports is usually very good and the documentation (e. g. description, glossary) is usually very comprehensive.
- **High number of indicators**: Reports are normally not limited to a manageable number of indicators (reports with over 50 KPIs from one singe process group could be identified). This has the advantage that the reports are able to provide accurate in-

formation for specific questions, but gaining an overview with regard to strategy fulfillment becomes difficult.

For analyzing the current situation at ABC, it is also necessary to consider the latest economic situation: Due to many political decisions in Austria, the company faces the challenge of changing markets and industries. At present, ABC is focusing on three basic efforts:

- First, the existing business needs to become more efficient and optimized in order to deliver cost-effective customer solutions.
- Second, international business will play an increasing role in the future for traditional products and services.
- Third, new business areas and business ideas (e. g. piping and control systems for block heating works), which fit strategically into the company's portfolio, will need to be realized.

The timing of the introduction of the BSC is thus just right: The company faces the challenge of adapting new strategies, and needs an effective and efficient new management concept that can support these change programs.

## 2.4  Context of the Implementation

ABC aimed to implement a BSC to establish an enterprise-wide strategy management and controlling. In order to take advantage of the learning effects of a pilot project, ABC decided to first launch a pilot project in order to generate initial experiences (see later ingredient 1). The ABC's central departments maintain intensive contact with all other departments. Therefore, the pilot application was realized in a corporate function because by this way a positive image of the BSC and interest in the concept can more easily spread within the whole enterprise.

The internal logistic process was selected for this trial run: The process is responsible for export, logistics and customs for all transportation of internal customers (e. g. the operational units of

ABC). The process team in charge acts as a connecting link between internal departments, which have national or international orders to transport goods to other places and logistics service providers such as UPS, DHL and Schenker, which perform the actual transport. The motivation of the process owner and team to implement a BSC is that so far no actual quality figures and performance indicators are available. Although core indicators such as the number of transports or transported kilometers of all goods are reported in order to underline the importance of the department, these figures are not suitable for assessing productivity or measuring the achievement of strategic goals. Moreover the logistics process acts in an important operational business area and must therefore provide comprehensive quality indicators for ISO certification. The new BSC should fill these gaps.

The application of the BSC in the sample scenario will thus be presented in the following chapters on two fundamental levels in order to support readers with different backgrounds:

- **Corporate level**: The developed ingredients were applied to the corporate company level of ABC. This presentation can be used by top managers and readers who are interested in the generic application of the BSC concept.
- **Process level**: The pilot application for the internal logistic process will be presented in detail. This presentation can be used by middle and lower managers as well by team leads and process owner to get deep insights into a very comprehensive and successful sample application of the BSC framework.

## 2.5   Starting Point for Cooking

Since the described scenario could be observed by the authors in many other cases and within many other companies, it is an excellent starting point for addressing best practices of BSCs in this cookbook: The company is basically willing to control strategy achievement using a framework but also wants to implement an IT-based lean system which is actionable for top managers as well as for heads of departments. Moreover a systematic redesign and modernization of the known reporting systems are necessary to transfer the framework from a pure and less meaningful controlling system to a modern and traceable framework to foster strategy implementation and controlling.

The following chapters will detail the described initial starting points presented above by using theoretical results but also by presenting concrete examples and hints.

# 3   Basic Recipe: The Original BSC Concept

| For the quick reader | |
| --- | --- |
| **Fundamental spice** | "Translating strategy into action", Kaplan and Norton 1992 |
| **The original in a nutshell** | The original BSC concept needs to be understood as sequential but flexible process-oriented approach: Coming from a long-term vision and strategic targets, the BSC develops indicators and actions, which are suitable for realizing short-term strategy implementation. |

In order to supply a basis for the ingredient later on, this chapter will outline the basics[3] of the BSC. Readers, who are already familiar with the basic recipe of starting with a vision, coming to strategic targets, KPIs and actions can skip this chapter and can directly go on with the ingredients.

## 3.1   History and Modern Definition

The idea of the BSC goes back to a research project conducted by the Professors Kaplan and Norton in twelve large-sized US companies in 1992. The basic assumption of their project was that existing

---

3   As the BSC concept is already well-documented, only major aspects, which are essential for the cooking recipe will be outlined. Should the reader be interested in a more detailed documentation of the BSC as a performance-oriented management system, please refer to Kaplan and Norton (1992), Kaplan and Norton (1993), Kaplan and Norton (1997), Kaplan and Norton (2001), Niven (2002) and Bible, Kerr and Zanini (2006).

concepts for ratio systems, which were, at the time, mainly based upon the conditions of industrial production, were no longer adequate for the issues of modern management like cooperation with suppliers and customers, customer segmentation, globalization, innovation and knowledge management (Kaplan and Norton 1997, pp. VIlff.). Major changes like cross-functional working, have significantly influenced and transformed the traditional budget-driven management systems. Kaplan and Norton looked for a well-balanced concept that combined long- as well as short-term targets, financial as well as non-financial indicators, leading as well as lagging indicators and internal as well as external perspectives (Kaplan and Norton 1997, pp. VIlff.; Kaplan and Norton 1997, pp. 7ff.; Ringe 2006, pp. 42ff.). These results shaped their pioneering article "The BSC – Measures that Drive Performance" in the Harvard Business Review 1992, where the BSC concept was published for the first time (Kaplan and Norton 1992).

Although the concept was at that time considered to be a fundamental innovation in controlling, it was nevertheless a continued development of already existing approaches. As early as 1959, Lauzel and Cibert described the **Tableau de Bord**, which is a concept along quite similar outlines.[4] Like the BSC, it is strategically focused, can be applied to all levels of a company and combines monetary as well as non-monetary indicators (Lauzel and Cibert 1959). Kaplan and Norton (1997, p. 28) dismiss the French concept as a mere compilation of success indicators.

The fact that the BSC is, in contrast to the Tableau de Bord, successful on an international level is usually contributed to the fact that its publishing medium (Harvard Business Review) has high distribution, that the authors were internationally acclaimed and that it was not only nationally available but also published in translation (Hoffmann 1999, p. 49; Barthélemy et al. 2010, pp. 59f.).

Since 1992, the BSC has been commonly recognized as a *performance measurement system* and differs from classical ratio systems in several aspects (see table 1). This book follows the defini-

---

4    For further details on this performance concept please refer to Lauzel and Cibert (1959).

tion of Gleich (2001, pp. 60ff.), who defines traditional ratio systems as a

> set of figures, which shows how different parameters are related, with the aim to create solid economical statements about companies.

Typical examples for traditional ratio systems are the well-known **DuPont** concept and the system of **ZVEI** (Gladen 2003, p. 92).

Table 1: Differences between ratio systems and performance management systems

| Criteria | Traditional ratio systems | Performance measurement systems |
|---|---|---|
| **Direction of all activities** | Short-term success | Long-term success |
| **Performance measurement** | One-dimensional, mainly financial | Multidimensional |
| **Focus** | Cost reduction | Overall performance |
| **Features of indicators** | ▪ Financial ▪ Historical ▪ Quantitative | ▪ Financial and non-financial ▪ Future-oriented ▪ Quantitative and qualitative |
| **Inspection and learning** | Isolated and individual (time, cost and quality) | Integrated and interconnected in terms of organization |
| **Connection with strategy** | None | Available as operationalization of strategies |

| Complexity | High | Low |
|---|---|---|
| Supplier of guidelines | Only top management | All parts of the organization |
| Demonstration of cause and effect | None | Available |
| Variance analysis | Insufficient | Assignment to individuals or areas is possible |
| Database | Accounting | All parts of the organization |

[Source: own illustration[5]]

Although initially Kaplan and Norton did not appreciate the implications of the BSC at the time (Kaplan and Norton 2001b), their general tendency to focus on business strategy motivated (and still explains) the success of the BSC later on. One major advantage of the BSC compared to other known concepts is that it manages to connect strategy to indicators and initiatives. Another advantage is the new idea of strategic management (Barthélemy et al. 2010, pp. 61ff.). Engel (2006, pp. 94ff.) describes this change as the latest evolutionary step in business administration and modern management literature. Modern literature usually views the use of strategic concepts such as the BSC instead of traditional ratio systems for management practice more favorably (Eicker, Kress and Lelke 2005, p. 4).

Nowadays, the BSC concept is regarded as one of the most important *performance management systems* (Sushil 2008, pp. 3f.), which is the reason why this concept is so successful (Othman et al. 2006). Today, Kaplan and Norton (1997, pp. 23f.) see their concept

---

5    The table is an own illustration and combines results from Peters (2008, p. 76), Engel (2006, p. 126), Müller (2000, p.65), Gleich (2001, pp. 6f.) and Gladen (2003, p. 128).

in contrast to static control systems as part of the continuous strategic management process (see figure 3) that translates a company's vision into organizational actions so as to ensure continuous learning.

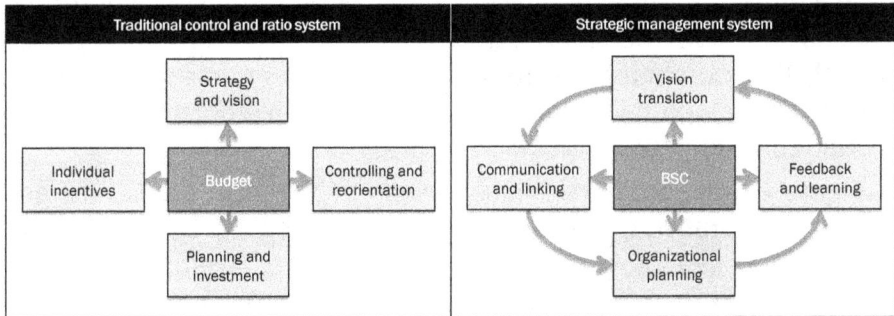

| Traditional control and ratio system | Strategic management system |
|---|---|
| Strategy and vision | Vision translation |
| Individual incentives / Budget / Controlling and reorientation | Communication and linking / BSC / Feedback and learning |
| Planning and investment | Organizational planning |

Figure 2: Comparison of traditional ratio systems and strategic management systems
[Source: own illustration adopted from Kaplan and Norton (1997, p. 23)]

Although a detailed and precise definition of the BSC is difficult due to continuous changes and the application to manifold usages (Ringe 2006, pp. 41f.), Kaplan and Norton (1997, pp. Vf.) try to describe their concept in a generic definition as a

> management system, which has the aim to define all, planning, performing and controlling processes in an enterprise.

However, this book and all ingredients will follow Niven (2002, p. 14) who defines the BSC in a broader way as a

- **Measurement system** helping organizations to translate its vision into objectives and indicators, as a
- **Strategic management system** supporting organizations in aligning short-term actions with their overall strategy, and as a
- **Communication tool** ensuring that the organization's strategy reaches the average employee.

## 3.2 The BSC as Process-oriented Approach

Summing up the history of their definitions, Kaplan and Norton (1996, pp. 75ff.) reached the conclusion that the BSC "addresses a serious deficiency in traditional management systems", namely the "inability to link a company's long-term strategy with its short-term actions" (Kaplan and Norton, 1996, pp. 75ff.). Moreover it is an approach that combines the traditional roots of financial key figures with performance measurement that reflects historical events with modern challenges.

Figure 3 unites different illustrations of the BSC procedure and shows the iterative overall BSC approach, which will be used in this research: Based on the vision and mission of a global company (chapter 3.2.1, p. 31), strategic objectives (chapter 3.2.3, p. 31) are developed within the four perspectives (chapter 3.2.2, p. 31). These objectives are then translated into specific actions (chapter 3.2.4, p. 34).

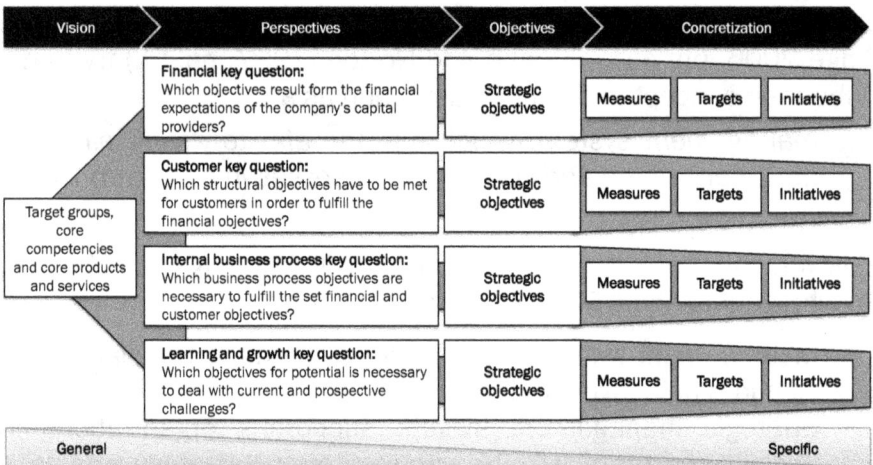

Figure 3: The BSC approach to translate vision into actions

[Source: own illustration adopted from Horvath & Partners (2007, p. 44); Horvath & Partners (2007, p. 68); Dressler (2004, pp. 222f.); Gaiser and Greiner (2002, p. 199)]

This chapter will look at the various stages of this approach in detail.

### 3.2.1 Vision

Before a BSC can be cooked, a company has to clarify its vision statement (often also called corporate vision). Usually, a company defines its favorite self-image based on the belief in an ideal idea of man and a perfect economic and social system (Schlögl 2003, p. 10). Often, the corporate vision as well as the mission, which can be interpreted as superior statements, are defined when the enterprise is founded. Both create the fundamental guidelines and policy for the enterprise in its entirety (Haunerdinger and Probst 2006, p. 22) as well as for all following steps in the BSC approach. In the case of ABC, a vision was already given:

> ABC wants to become the world leader in design, installation, maintenance and deconstruction of oil-based power plants as well as of manufacturing plants for fluid chemicals.

According to Kaplan and Norton (1997, p. 23) most modern companies formulated mission statements in order to communicate basic values and fundamental views to all employees. Missions should normally state target groups, core competencies and major product lines or services.

### 3.2.2 Perspectives

Based on their empirical studies from 1992, Kaplan and Norton proved that most successful companies manage to balance four perspectives (see figure 5) successfully (Kaplan and Norton 1997, pp. 8ff.; Horvath & Partners 2007, pp. 41f.):

- **Financial perspective**: This perspective indicates the real success in traditional return-oriented companies. It documents the final goals of business activities, namely the long-term financial business success.
- **Customer perspective**: This perspective concentrates on the appearance and position in the market. The organization formulates which benefit has to be supplied in order to fulfill customer needs.

- **Business processes perspective**: Measures in this perspective have to define required outputs of core business processes in order to guarantee customer and financial targets.
- **Learning and growth perspective**: This perspective is to build up and maintain the necessary strategic infrastructure including employees, knowledge, innovation, creativity, technology, and information as resources. In contrast to the other perspectives, the learning and growth perspective aims to ensure continuing change and adjustment to future market requirements.

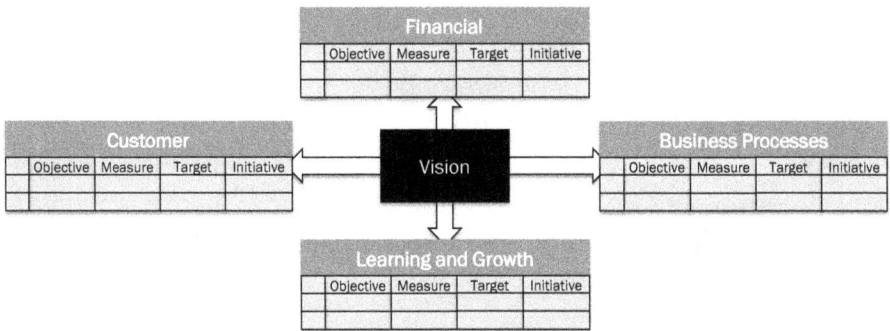

Figure 4: Four perspectives of the BSC
[Source: own illustration adopted from Kaplan and Norton (1996)]

Kaplan and Norton provide key questions (see figure 4) that can lead to actual strategic objectives in each perspective.

### 3.2.3 Objectives

In the BSC concept, a strategy is understood to consist of hypotheses about the interrelation of causes and effects (Kaplan and Norton 1997, p. 28). Strategic objectives are documented in formal and clear written text-form (Horvath and Kaufmann 1998, pp. 6ff.; Girmscheid 2006, p. 149). According to Horvath & Partners (2007, pp. 156ff.) the creation of strategic objectives consists of two fundamental steps.

First the mission is translated into strategic objectives which include the deduction, selection and concentration of many possible objectives based on the company's vision (Horvath & Partners 2007, pp. 156ff.). The strategy therefore contains both goals and a planned roadmap (Barthélemy et al. 2010, p. 65). After clarifying its meaning and strategic importance, all strategic objectives are documented with the corresponding perspective and a written description (Horvath & Partners 2007, pp. 156ff.).

After their original BSC concept, Kaplan and Norton (2001, p. 63) published the idea of a strategy map and defined this new framework as structure for the full description of a strategy. That means that with a strategy map, the selected strategic objects are integrated into cause and effect chains (Horvath & Partners 2007, pp.186f.). Figure 5 shows the example of a strategy map for the afore-mentioned Hungarian case study. As the example indicates, a strategy map allows a very clear presentation of the most important cause-and-effect relationships relevant to their implementation goals with each other (Umbeck, Lederer and Nitze 2009, pp. 390f.). Although only the causal connection of objectives can generate a full understanding of a strategy, many companies do not yet use strategy maps. This is why Speckbacher, Bischof and Pfeiffer (2003, p. 363) describe the strategy map as one major and essential evolutionary step in the implementation of a BSC.

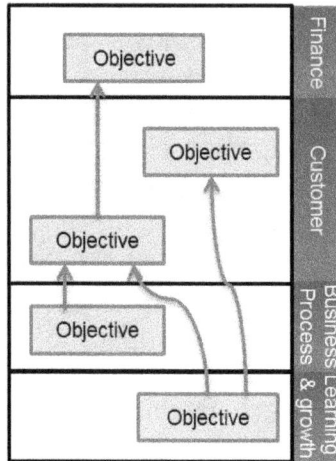

Figure 5: Schema of a strategy map
[Source: own illustration adopted from Kaplan and Norton 1997]

## 3.2.4 Refinement

After defining the strategic objectives, they must be clarified with indicators, targets, and initiatives. In their analysis Paranjape, Rossiter and Pantano (2006, pp. 4ff.) came to the conclusion that this part of the BSC approach is the most difficult but also the most success-critical in practice.

The strategic goals should be formulated so that corresponding indicators can be determined (König and Rehling 2002, p. 7). Measures should indicate the success rate of strategy implementation and execution (Wunder 2001, p. 137). Based on the indicators it should be possible to understand the rate of goal achievement and it must be possible to lead employees according to the corporate strategy (Wickel-Kirsch 2001, pp. 281f.).

Once the targets for measures are documented, actions must be defined that ensure the achievement of targets (König and Rehling 2002, pp. 7f.) and therefore the achievement of the strategy.

# 4    Recipe for a Successful BSC

## 4.1    Ingredient 1: Planning and Introduction

| For the quick reader | |
| --- | --- |
| **Fundamental spice** | "The BSC introduction must be seen as a strategic change project.", Bauer 2012 |
| **Ingredient 1 in a nutshell** | This first ingredient deals with all aspects necessary for the introduction of a BSC which need to be set up in advance. The targets behind the BSC need to be addressed first. Then the actual implementation needs to be rolled out as a project following a best practice introduction process. Many experiences show that the launch of a pilot project before a comprehensive implementation can help to prevent typical mistakes. |

### 4.1.1 Definition

The first ingredient requires a systematic planning as well as introduction of the whole approach. Sources in research publications, especially reports by experts, describe the ex-ante work on the BSC approach as particularly important. The name **introduction and planning** was chosen because initially, the aspects involved here concentrate on the preliminary design of actions (such as setting the overall objectives for the BSC project, planning a rollout strategy, design of responsibilities and procedures) as well as on their execution (in a particular pilot test run, for example). Both aspects can range from implementation to a continuous process.

Soft factors such as awareness raising (PricewaterhouseCoopers n.d.), corporate culture (Hyperspace 2010), acceptance of external consulting (Hyperspace 2010; Crespo et al. 2009), knowledge transfer (Niven 2002; Mair 2002; Blackall 2007; Morisawa and Kurosaki 2003) and motivation (Schmeisser and Clausen 2009) can also play a major role in this ingredient. For instance, all presented parts of the recipe are not to be seen as isolated but positively influence each other. Nevertheless, these soft aspects will be systematically addressed in ingredient 5 (*Acceptance and Support*).

### 4.1.2 Background

"Tell me how your project starts and I will tell you how it ends" is a statement often quoted in management literature. It demonstrates the importance of planning in general. Known reports and studies also emphasize the importance of planning for a BSC project in general, and often give specific instructions and advice as well.

### 4.1.3 Components

Figure 6 depicts the ingredient's components: Before the initiation of a BSC project, the management needs to clarify for which purposes and goals a BSC will be introduced (Morisawa and Kurosaki 2003; Vohl 2004). Numerous references recommend a pilot run of the BSC before the organization-wide roll out in a selected area of the company (Schmeisser and Clausen 2009; Pandey 2005; Williams 2004). Findings from this test run can then be used in the following implementation process (Horvath & Partners 2007, pp. 156ff.; Schmeisser and Clausen 2009; Blackall 2007). This step contributes to the successful implementation of the developed BSC approach and also includes two additional ingredients (i. e. ingredient 3, cascading, and ingredient 2, integration). The introduction needs to be supported by a project management (Weber and Schäffer 2000).

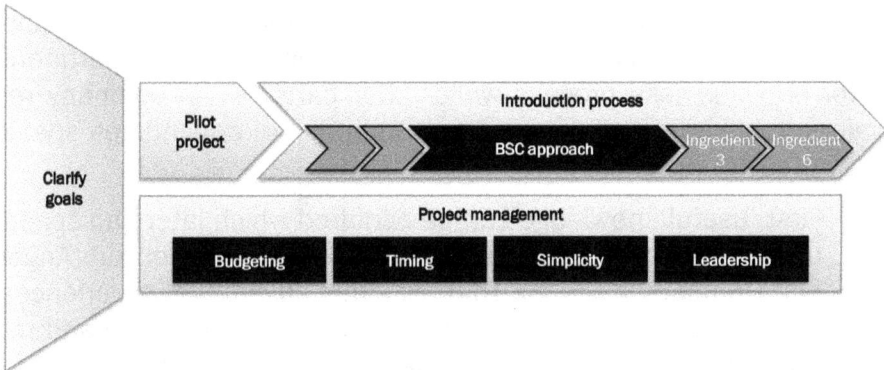

Figure 6: Components of the ingredient introduction and planning
[Source: own illustration]

In detail the ingredient is realized by the four components **clarification of goals, realization of a pilot project, introduction process** and **project management.**

### Clarification of Goals

Lawson, Stratton and Hatch (2006) request that a BSC should only be implemented if appropriate reasons for the implementation have been established. Therefore, the motivation to use a BSC project has to be discussed and explicitly documented (Morisawa and Kurosaki 2003). Often a time-consuming analysis and re-fitting of the BSC approach is necessary (Vohl 2004). Scope, objectives, guidelines and requirements for the overall project should be determined in advance (Weber and Schäffer 2000). This should take place even before a general project management is assigned to the task. In addition, all findings from this preliminary run as well as necessary assumptions about the introduction (Hyperspace 2010) should be previously communicated (Bauer 2010).

### Pilot Project

Several experience and expert reports recommend a pilot application at an early stage. This test run has the purpose to pave the way for the BSC at all organizational levels (Pandey 2005; McCunn 1998). The BSC can at first be implemented in only one department or for one business process while other parts of the company remain untouched at this point. Two fundamental advantages speak in favor of this approach:

- First, useful knowledge can be acquired which later can speed up and support the successful organization-wide roll out (Angel and Rampersad 2005). To realize this advantage, experiences must be gained (for example from a group of experts) and re-applied (Morisawa and Kurosaki 2003; Angel and Rampersad 2005).
- Second, the positive experiences from a successful test run can increase the acceptance throughout the enterprise (see also ingredient 5, *Acceptance and Support*).

In order to set up a successful pilot application, the company needs a reliable failure culture (PricewaterhouseCoopers n.d.) as well as high resource endowment (Hyperspace 2010).

### Introduction Process

After clarifying the underlying reasons for the introduction and after a successful pilot application, the actual organizational implementation process can start. Reports supply numerous proposals on how a correct implementation process has to be performed in practice. Often the basic steps are similar, but some slight variations in details can be observed. McCunn (1998) and Crespo et al. (2009) describe that the company's strategy notifies the beginning of the process. Angel and Rampersad (2005) and Crespo et al. (2009) propose a flexible process with various degrees of freedom, because many unexpected events can occur in the management project. Nevertheless, Schmeisser and Clausen (2009) ask for a process which includes detailed plans for cost and time in each phase.

Blackall (2007) points out that in general a suitable sequence of the implementation steps is important.

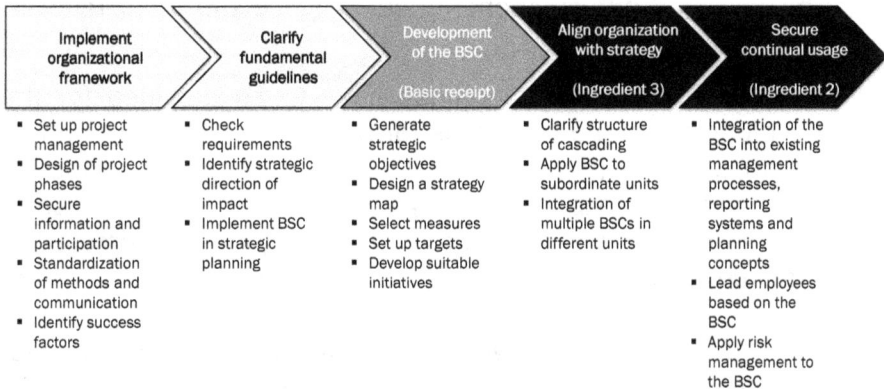

| Implement organizational framework | Clarify fundamental guidelines | Development of the BSC (Basic receipt) | Align organization with strategy (Ingredient 3) | Secure continual usage (Ingredient 2) |
|---|---|---|---|---|
| • Set up project management<br>• Design of project phases<br>• Secure information and participation<br>• Standardization of methods and communication<br>• Identify success factors | • Check requirements<br>• Identify strategic direction of impact<br>• Implement BSC in strategic planning | • Generate strategic objectives<br>• Design a strategy map<br>• Select measures<br>• Set up targets<br>• Develop suitable initiatives | • Clarify structure of cascading<br>• Apply BSC to subordinate units<br>• Integration of multiple BSCs in different units | • Integration of the BSC into existing management processes, reporting systems and planning concepts<br>• Lead employees based on the BSC<br>• Apply risk management to the BSC |

Figure 7: Best practice introduction process

[Source: own illustration, phase process based on Horvath & Partners (2007, p. 74)]

The five-phase process developed by Horvath & Partners (2007, pp. 74ff.) is primarily applied in business practice and frequently used in different case studies and can therefore be seen as best practice process. Figure 7 shows a simplified variation of this process: In addition to the original model, the phases shown here point out that the third phase of the process corresponds to the presented BSC approach from the basic recipe. The last two phases of the approach basically correspond to ingredient 2 and 3.

### Project Management

Project management plays an essential role in the implementation of a BSC (Weber and Schäffer 2000). Usually, management is project-oriented, which implies a focus on one-time solutions to reach clearly defined goals. The introduction is usually temporary, with the implementation planned for a limited period of time, since continuing operation requires continuous processes (see also ingredient 6, *Continuous Process*). Similar to most projects, teamwork is a vital aspect of BSC implementation projects (Morisawa and Kurosaki 2003). Typically, projects face a high degree of uncertainty. This is true for BSC introduction projects as well (Angel and Rampersad 2005; Crespo et al. 2009). It can be concluded that the management of a BSC introduction is indeed like the management of a project. The following sub-components seem to be the most relevant factors for project success:

- **Budgeting**: Sufficient resources have to be provided for the development stage as well as for project management and pilot applications (Hyperspace 2010; McCunn 1998). Although the amount of expenses is highly dependent on the case in question, the necessary budget is usually underestimated in practice (Value Competence Consulting 2002; McCunn 1998). During the allocation process (see also ingredient 2, *Integration*), the project manager works towards having the project approved and secures the necessary financial resources. By carefully planning the budget, project managers may avoid a premature end of BSC implementations just after the implementation phase has concluded (Hyperspace 2010).
- **Timing**: The timing and timespan allowed for the launch is critical for success (Niven 2002). Often, BSC implementation projects are started without sufficient time for preparation and results are expected too soon (Crespo et al. 2009).
- **Simplicity**: A high level of uncertainty is typical for the beginning / start of a project. A high level of uncertainty is typical for the beginning / start of a project (Zell 2008, p. 5). This means in the case of a BSC introduction that very often not all necessary data is available at start (Angel and Rampersad 2005). In addition, some management tasks cannot be planned at the beginning (Crespo et al. 2009). This implies for successful project management that it is highly recommended to focus on pragmatic aspects rather than to aim at immediate perfection (McCunn 1998). This includes focusing on core areas for implementation (Vohl 2004). At an early stage, the complexity should be reduced to an acceptable minimum. In later phases (see also ingredient 6), when underlying processes are stabilized, the BSC can be refined and enhanced.
- **Leadership**: Project management needs leadership. This means for a BSC that the employees in charge must be skilled

in their field. Promoters are necessary to drive the project with their expertise (Hyperspace 2010). Leaders serve as multipliers and need to have expertise (Mair 2002), acquired knowledge (Blackall 2007), and a full understanding of the functions of a BSC (Angel and Rampersad, 2005). The lack of methodological knowledge and expertise of leading managers is one of the main reasons for failure during the implementation stage (Niven 2002). Morisawa and Kurosaki (2003) recommend to manage the BSC by a separate organizational team or a central business unit consisting of trained experts. In order to achieve good leadership, deploying external consulting is considered to be necessary by many authors (Crespo et al. 2009; Hyperspace 2010; Schmeisser and Clausen 2009; Bauer 2010). Even if external consultants imply higher costs (Crespo et al. 2009) and cooperation with external experts needs awareness building (Hyperspace 2010), an external consultant adds two fundamental advantages (Crespo et al. 2009): External specialists provide new impulses for discussion and can create a new point of view. In addition, the adjusting company will benefit from a methodological and substantial knowledge transfer.

### 4.1.4 Advantages

All in all, the implementation of all components offers several advantages; some were already mentioned in the component descriptions. The most important advantages of this ingredient seem to be:

- Knowledge building and clarification of basic policies will pay off more than once during a long BSC operation. Without a binding introduction process, subsequent corrections will generate expensive and complicated changes afterwards.
- The use of a successful pilot application can generate a positive attitude towards the BSC and supply an important knowledge base, which can later help to speed up and facilitate the organization-wide rollout (Weber and Schäffer 2000).

- Like in any other project, management, including budgeting, leadership and process responsibility, are essential factors for a holistic success (Weber and Schäffer 2000).

### 4.1.5 Limitations and Restrictions

Using a widespread design for the BSC project seems only to be reasonable if high investments will pay off, meaning a long-term operation is planned.

The degree of intensity has to be determined for all components. For example research explicitly states the balance between a fixed and binding implementation process and a flexible handling of the introduction (Crespo et al. 2009; Angel and Rampersad 2005). Moreover, it is suggested that external consultants should not merely try to implement initiatives of their own, but should only act as ad-hoc support (Bauer 2010).

### 4.1.6 Introduction

Since this ingredient outlines the introduction of a BSC, further description of the introduction is not necessary.

### 4.1.7 Example of Application

#### Corporate Level

In a first step, the corporate BSC of ABC needed to be well planned.

*Clarification of Goals*

The management board and senior managers of ABC could provide information on the goals of a possible BSC introduction as well as the requirements for implementation. To clarify the purposes, inter-

nal workshops were conducted. The outcoming goals and requirements are shown on the left side in figure 8.

| Goals of ABC | Support by strategy-focused approaches | | |
|---|---|---|---|
| | Performance Pyramid | Performance Prism | BSC |
| A strategy instrument has to be established, which can contribute to the business success of ABC in a systematic and traceable way. | Fully | Fully | Fully<br>Can be secured by the BSC approach. |
| All necessary information about the current state of the business and the most important figures must be seen and interpreted at a glance. | Partly | Partly | Fully<br>Information is aggregated to one single card. Only key points are presented. |
| The new concept is to communicate the strategy of ABC to leaders, employees and external stakeholders. | Partly | Fully | Fully<br>A stated goal of the BSC is strategy communication and transparency (e.g. with the help of strategy maps). |
| The new framework should realize a general approach, in which each strategy can be operationalized within ABC, independent of its actual contents. | Partly | Partly | Fully<br>Can be secured by the BSC approach and the integration into existing frameworks. |
| The new concept has to provide comparative (e.g. time series) or at least comparable (e.g. by benchmarking) data. | Partly | Partly | Partly<br>The basic receipt does not include these aspects, but they can be incorporated into the architecture. |
| The overall strategy of ABC is expected to be broken down into consistent individual actions. The strategy should be systematically adapted to the departments. | Fully | Fully | Fully<br>This is a stated goal of the BSC, which can be achieved for example by the principle of cascading. |
| The new system should ensure that all activities result form strategy and a conclusion regarding the achievement of the strategy is possible. | Fully | Partly | Fully<br>Secured by the BSC approach and strategic feedback because the BSC differs form traditional ratio systems. |

Figure 8: Expectation and goals of top management and
analysis how different frameworks can solve these requirements
[Source: own illustration]

The central question before implementation of a BSC is whether the
expectations and goals of top management will be met within this
framework. The BSC can be grouped into the category of **strategy-
focused framework approaches,** where other management concepts
such as Performance Pyramid[6] and Performance Prism[7] are known
as well (Krause 2006, p.85ff.).

The right part of figure 8 looks at how these concepts can potentially deal with the described goals of ABC. It was confirmed as a result, that the BSC is indeed the best choice out of these frameworks

---

6    Detailed information about this concept can be found in Cross and Lynch 1998.

7    Detailed information about this concept can be found in Neely and Adams 2002.

to provide a solution taking the goals and requirements of ABC top management into account.

*Pilot Project*

In ingredient 1, the importance of a pilot project is emphasized. The pilot implementation of a BSC is recommended to generate important experiences and knowledge. Besides these goals, a pilot project can be used to gain a positive image of the BSC before a company-wide rollout.

Due to this reason, a BSC was implemented for the internal logistic process. This pilot run followed the six best practices of this book for the actual introduction and implementation.

*Project Management*

Ingredient 1 outlines the importance of project management, meaning that project management activities are necessary for the planning and implementation of the BSC at ABC in the first two years (see figure 21).

The necessary budget for the implementation of the corporate BSC is primarily allocated to the internal quality department because it acts as a **shared service** and supports the entire organization of ABC. As the implementation plan recommends an introduction in three years (see Figure 9), it probably also makes sense to estimate and document budget for this periods based on the specific recommendations given in each phase.

Figure 9 shows the recommendation for a comprehensive implementation of the BSC for ABC. Beginning in the first year, the BSC is used in one process to generate in-house knowledge and to establish a generally positive image. Experiences from this application will be used for the entire project planning at the corporate level. The **test runs** at each level indicate that although the BSC is already in use at this level, some aspects, such as full integration, risk management and continuous improvement are not yet established. In this phase, for example, aspects such as learning by doing are still possible and integration into the incentive system is not yet desired. Finally, during the phases of the **live operation** the BSC is fully conducted with all activities of the BSC approach and all developed ingredients.

After a six-month test run of the BSC at the corporate level, the management board can make a final decision whether the full rollout of the BSC concept should be implemented. If this decision is positive, the cascading process in which the BSC is applied to all lower levels of the company, such as HR, can start. From the beginning of the third year, the BSC is in use at all company levels.

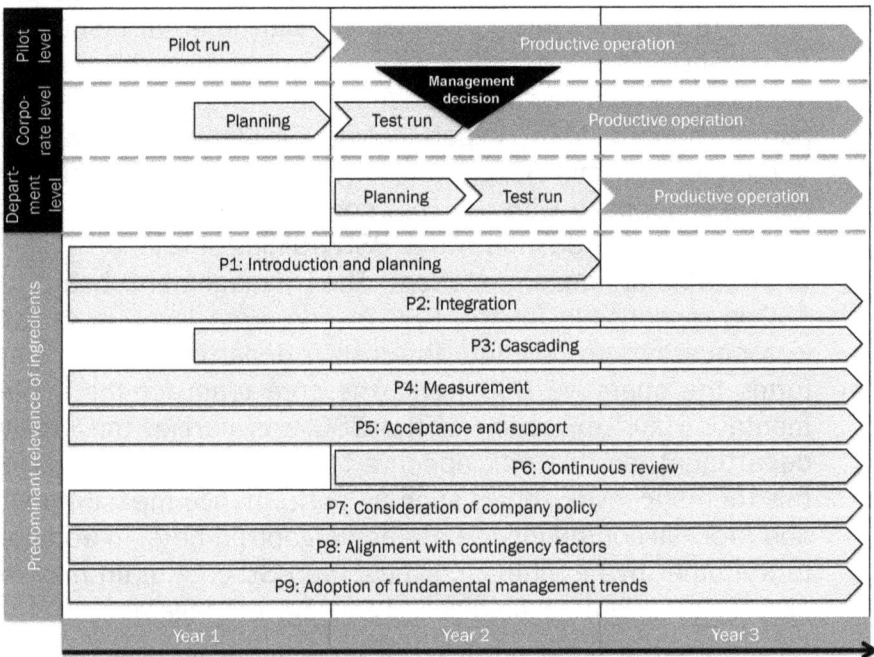

Figure 9: Overall time planning for BSC rollout
[Source: own illustration]

This schedule takes the findings of ingredient 1 into account, namely the necessity for the detailed planning and timing of a BSC. This is the reason why the full first year is reserved solely for the acquisition of knowledge and corporate planning. Ingredient 1 however also explains that the actual implementation has to take be performed fast and systematically. This is guaranteed by the short six-month test implemented at the corporate level.

Project management for the introduction of the BSC must be equipped with suitable leadership from the quality department. With respect to the recommendations in ingredient 1, the following recommendations can be made for ABC:

- **Consulting**: The recommendation is to use external consultancy to support the rollout. However, this is not suitable in the case of ABC. In the tradition of the company, such change projects are usually realized completely with internal resources. As acceptance of external advice will not be high, it is recommended that in-house knowledge is made available in a transparent manner. Many experts could be identified at various departments within ABC. Many of these people have already gained experience with the BSC concept during their careers, or have participated in previous BSC training sessions.
- **Organizational implementation**: The management board of ABC is responsible for the BSC at corporate level. In fact, it was necessary to delegate tasks to a department which performs the operative BSC work. The core team for the implementation and execution of the BSC was part of the quality department, as this unit appears to be most appropriate for this thematic level. Topics such as performance measurement and process controlling are already organized here. In addition to the other five existing activities, the BSC core team may realize a new operative field called *strategy management*.

*Introduction Process*

For the implementation process, which took place according to overall planning in the second half of the first year, four meetings were planned (see figure 23). These meetings followed the developed BSC approach: Before operating the corporate BSC in a test run, the strategy of ABC had to be defined (first BSC workshop) and then assigned to indicators and target values (second BSC workshop). In the third workshop, a BSC implementation plan was developed.

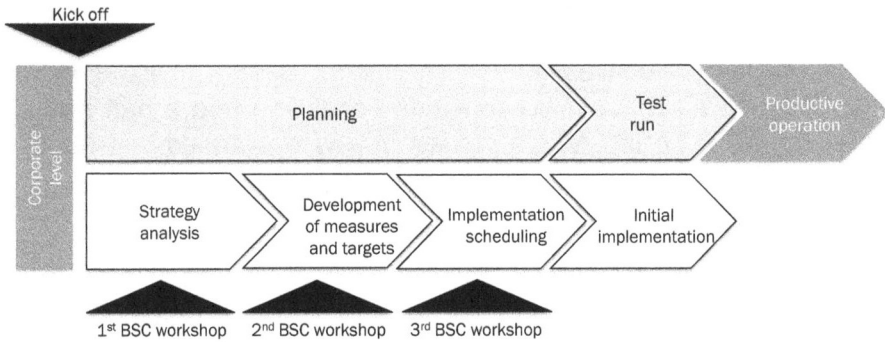

Figure 10: Proposal for the introduction process of the corporate BSC with kick-off and three BSC workshops

[Source: own illustration]

The introduction process started with a formal **kick-off**, which was organized primarily for information and team-building purposes. A developed outline including participants, agenda, documents and materials of this meeting can be found in Appendix A.1. All stakeholders have been informed about the project plans, received information about the key objectives and got a first impression of the introduction schedule. Additionally, top management presented the vision of ABC:

*ABC wants to become the world leader in design, installation, maintenance and deconstruction of oil-based power plants as well as of manufacturing plants for fluid chemicals.*

In addition to these more business-related objectives, sustainability (i.e. safety, security and environmental protection), in general is also another primary aim of ABC. This fundamental decision results from the particular branch: The chemical industry, in which ABC operates, is highly under pressure to follow regulations for environmental protection and nature conservation. Incidents or offenses can have such an impact that these aspects play an equally large role as economic goals.

Before the first BSC workshop, in which participants worked on specific results, it was recommended that **strategy interviews** are conducted: This modified Delphi method provided the basis for discussion during the first BSC workshop. The interviews were not designed for a long discussion but were primarily used to collect possible strategic objectives for the workshop. Based on experiences from this project it could be concluded that one and a half hour is sufficient for such interviews. An agenda with detailed instructions to perform these interviews is provided in Appendix A.2.

This modified Delphi method had two key advantages:

- The naming of strategic objectives (in the strategy interviews) was separated from their evaluation (in the first BSC workshop). This means that both majority opinions as well as important individual aspects were discussed in the workshop.
- This approach minimized the required time for the collection of important objectives. If the strategic objectives were developed in the first BSC workshop, managers would perhaps unnecessarily spend a lot of time in meetings.

The aggregated results of the strategy interviews were presented in the first workshop. Individual issues have been discussed and the participants developed a common strategy map at the corporate level. A recommended guideline for this first BSC workshop is provided in appendix A.3.

The **elaboration of indicators and initiatives** was carried out in the second BSC workshop (a detailed recommendation for a suitable agenda is provided in appendix A.4) in small groups in order to guarantee concentrated work within a reasonable time. Each group focused on one BSC perspective and had two days for preparation. The work was methodically supported by the experts from the strategy management and was documented using the provided forms (appendix A.5). During the processing period, the groups had the opportunity to meet, discuss and conduct research in the workshop rooms or in their departments or process teams.

For all the strategic objectives, the **strategic objective documentation forms** that document the resulting indicators, targets and initiatives was completed (appendix A.5). As completing the form required various skill sets, the small groups was arranged in a cross-functional manner.

Finally, the team leaders of each small group presented the contents of their perspective. The presentation order was bottom-up and the consistency of the overall results needed to be checked as part of an open discussion at the end of the workshop: Indicators, targets and responsibilities could have been added, modified or deleted until the results have had reached an acceptable solution for the majority of participants.

| | | Process A | | | Process B | | | | Pr. C | | Process D | | | Process E | | |
|---|---|---|---|---|---|---|---|---|---|---|---|---|---|---|---|---|
| | | Initiative 1 | Initiative 2 | Initiative 3 | Initiative 4 | Initiative 5 | Initiative 6 | Initiative 7 | Initiative 8 | Initiative 9 | Initiative 10 | Initiative 11 | Initiative 12 | Initiative 13 | Initiative 14 | Initiative 15 |
| Financial | Strategic objective 1 | | ■ | | ■ | ■ | | ■ | ■ | | | ■ | | ■ | ■ | |
| | Strategic objective 2 | | | | | ■ | | | | | | | | | | |
| | Strategic objective 3 | ■ | | | | | ■ | | | | | ■ | | | | |
| Sustainability | Strategic objective 4 | | | | | | | | | | | | | | | |
| | Strategic objective 5 | | | ■ | ■ | | | | ■ | ■ | ■ | | | | | ■ |
| | Strategic objective 6 | | | | | | ■ | | | | | | | | | |
| Partner | Strategic objective 7 | | | | | ■ | | | ■ | | | | | ■ | | |
| | Strategic objective 8 | | ■ | | | | | | | | | | | | | |
| Business processes | Strategic objective 9 | ■ | | | | | ■ | | | | | | | ■ | ■ | |
| | Strategic objective 10 | | | | | ■ | ■ | ■ | ■ | ■ | ■ | ■ | | | | |
| | Strategic objective 11 | | | | | | ■ | ■ | | | | | | | | |
| | Strategic objective 12 | | ■ | | | | | ■ | | | | | | | | |
| Learning & growth | Strategic objective 13 | ■ | | | | | | | ■ | | | | ■ | | | |
| | Strategic objective 14 | | | ■ | ■ | | | | | | | | | | | |
| | Strategic objective 15 | | | | | | | | ■ | ■ | | | | | | ■ |

Figure 11: Template for an initiative map at corporate level

[Source: own illustration]

One central output of this workshop was a so-called **initiative map** (Figure 12). This schedule aimed to combine the various strategic objectives within the perspectives[8] with the assigned responsibilities (level of processes). At the same time, this map sets the stage for cascading to the next level of ABC: The initiatives from this map must be understood as compulsory input for the cascaded department BSC in addition to the department's own further objectives.

In the third and last workshop, the strategy management team presented a consolidated version of the initiative map to refresh the results of the last workshop. In addition, the procedure for further integration (ingredient 2) and cascading (ingredient 3) was explained to those in charge of departments or processes. Additionally hints e.g. how to perform test runs in the process were offered. For this purpose **BSC experts** (see ingredient 6, *Acceptance and Support*) have been used in this parts of the training.

Moreover, the strategy management team provided a detailed schedule for year two and three of the implementation plan (see Figure 9) and put it up for discussion.

After the third meeting, two fundamental points were communicated: First, it is expected that the departments and process responsibles present current and future activities by using their BSC (e. g. in the senior management committee meetings) from the middle of the second year. Second, the department and process teams should know that central strategy management could support their work in implementing the BSC.

### Process Level

In the case of the logistic process, the kick-off meeting was organized by the quality department as proposed above. Fundamental aspects and questions have been addressed with the head of the

---

8    As it can be seen in Figure 12, the BSC of ABC used other perspectives than the original concept by Kaplan and Norton. These five perspectives are explained in detail in the application of ingredient 7. However, for further reading, it is not necessary, to first look at ingredient 7. It is sufficient to understand that in case of ABC, these five different perspectives are used.

department who was at the same time the process owner (e. g. get to know each other, presentation of the research project, motivation for introducing the BSC, definition of responsibilities).

Regarding the proposals for the introduction of the corporate BSC process, three BSC workshops were also carried out at the level of the pilot process. In detail, minor deviations were necessary (e. g. in the first workshop, the vision of the departments needed to be developed and strategy interviews were coordinated in the kick-off meeting or via a telephone conference). A team leader and employees from the logistics department attended each workshop meeting.

The following vision was developed and reviewed for the logistics process:

> The logistics process understands itself as internal logistics provider and strives for the highest possible internal customer satisfaction. This aim will be achieved by a zero-defect culture in which all transportation activities are implemented according to customers' requirements, namely to provide service that ensures that goods arrive at the right time, at the right quality and at the right place.

Thus, a comprehensive strategy map (see appendix A.12) was documented as well as indicators and initiatives were developed. A key activity in setting up the strategy maps consisted of a focus on the most important aspects: It was necessary to implement a Delphi study to prioritize the strategic goals.

The various templates developed in this book (appendix A) could be further improved in reviews and workshops. By doing so, the following steps such as the corporate BSC rollout and the rollout in other processes could benefit from optimized forms and lessons learned on how to organize and fill-out these templates in an efficient way.

The project management of both pilot projects was organized by the quality department and the documented components from ingredient 1 were in particular taken into account: The experts were responsible for the overall coordination and leadership of the workshops. In order to motivate and increase the acceptance of the new measurement system, some successful BSC examples from business practices were presented and participants committed on the main results of this research.

The employees appreciated that the quality department acted as an external consultant in the workshops, investigating existing business processes and thus was able to discover optimization opportunities together with the employees of the departments.

## 4.2   Ingredient 2: Integration

| For the quick reader | |
| --- | --- |
| **Fundamental spice** | "Deploy appropriate budgeting, IT, communication and reward systems.", Hendricks, Menor and Wiedmann, 2004 |
| **Ingredient 2 in a nutshell** | A BSC cannot exist, if it is separated from existing strategy processes, incentive systems, controlling and reporting activities as well as from allocation and risk management processes. A successful BSC needs to go along with frameworks in place but can of course influence and change the existing systems. |

### 4.2.1 Definition

The ingredient *Integration* describes the efforts to incorporate the BSC with existing or to be implemented concepts and frameworks within the company's organizational system. The general integration into other corporate systems, such as information processes, business activities and incentive schemes (Bodmer and Völker 2000), is particularly important (Peters 2008) but at the same time very challenging (Ghosh and Mukherjee 2006).

### 4.2.2 Background

As early as 1969, Chandler supported the idea that "a new strategy required a new or at least a refashioned structure if (...) [the company] was to be operated efficiently" (Chandler 1969, p. 15). The BSC can neither exist as an isolated concept nor unrelated to the company and its established frameworks and management practices (Hyperspace 2010; Bauer 2010). In order to avoid unilateral or isolated application and the disadvantages associated with a BSC, it should be holistically integrated into the organization. Kaplan and Norton (2001) promoted the idea of aligning the organization with the strategy and with all existing organizational concepts to put the concept to work.

### 4.2.3 Components

The systems within an organization in which the BSC can be integrated will be considered as components that work together to generate the overall success. The BSC should be integrated into strategy processes, information technology, incentive systems, controlling and reporting, allocation processes and risk management.

#### Strategy Process

Many sources from research literature clearly emphasize the relationship of the BSC to individual phases of the strategic management process. The BSC should be taken into account already at the stage of strategic planning (Pandey 2005) and review workshops of strategic targets are essential for the BSC success (Bodmer and Völker 2000).

Considering this ingredient, it seems to be recommendable to combine the entire strategic management process with the BSC. This assessment is shared by the research literatur. Figure 12 links the basic BSC recipe (chapter 3) to the generic strategic management process (Haid 2003, p. 16).

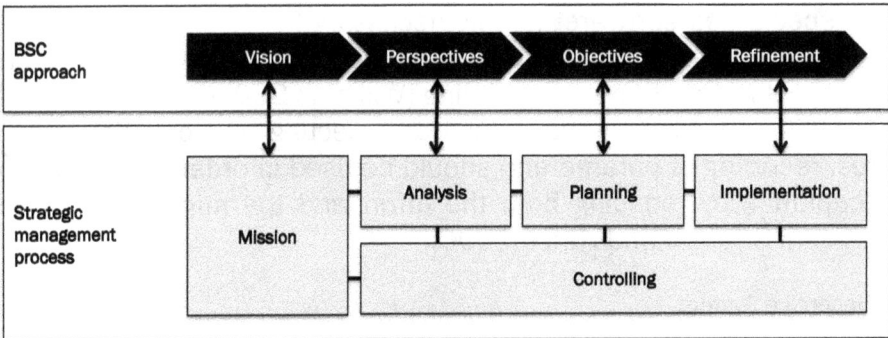

Figure 12: Integration of a BSC into the strategic management process
[Source: own illustration, partly adopted from Haid (2003, p. 16)]

It becomes clear that the BSC approach follows the basic strategic management phases. Kaplan and Norton (1997, pp. 142ff.) describe the BSC as an instrument to show, control and support the strategy process. The BSC can be brought to life if it is used in all business strategy meetings (Bauer 2010). As the BSC generates the opportunity to communicate a certain strategy and to lead managers to a common understanding of the strategic management process, this proceeding can be described as **management by discussion** (Horvath and Kaufmann 1998, p. 8).

Although the management process should be predominant (Ringe 2006, pp. 50ff.), Kaplan and Norton (1997, p. 156) describe their concept as an important instrument to translate the company's strategy into specific actions to support the overall policy. The specific design of the integration steps depends on the particular configuration of an organization's strategic management processes.

### Information Technology

Although the BSC cannot be an IT-driven concept, supporting technology is nevertheless a major factor (Williams 2004; Schermann and Volcic 2009; Bauer 2010). During the first steps of introduction, standard office software solutions suffice (Preißner 2007, p. 14) and specialized software[9] is only necessary for complex and enterprise-wide projects (Bauer 2010). IT technologies should be used primarily for reporting and analyzing (Williams 2004). In any case, all possibilities for automation (such as selecting and calculating figures, reporting of parameters) should be used in order to increaceto acceptance by reducing both the effort and the number of errors (Lawson, Stratton and Hatch 2006).

### Incentive System

The combination with an incentive system works in two directions: On the one hand, a rewarding concept can ensure that the BSC objectives will be achieved by extrinsic motivation (Hendricks, Menor and Wiedmann 2004). It is often proposed that the objectives of the BSC should be used for individual or group-based goal setting for employees (Bauer 2010) and for the distribution of bonuses depending on the actual success rate (Bodmer and Völker 2000).

On the other hand, the BSC can be used by employees as a template for their daily work (Angel and Rampersad 2005). Like this, the company's strategy is translated into concrete and precise steps (Kaplan and Norton 1997, pp. 156ff.). In that case, employees become accountable for their contribution (Niven 1998). It is recommended to increase the link to an incentive system step by step, as during the first learning-phase failures and errors in the usage of the BSC should not have negative consequences for individual employees (PricewaterhouseCoopers n.d.).

### Controlling and Reporting

Since a BSC is able to reveal strategy achievement, correctness and completion of key actions and as it uncovers the link to strategy, its close connection to reporting and controlling is often described as success factor (Broccardo 2010, p. 90). Nevertheless, a BSC should definitely not aim to replace already existing information processes or reporting mechanisms. In contrast to formal controlling, the BSC

---

9    For detailed information, case studies and best practices for IT-based BSCs, the readers should refer to Preuss (2002).

has to be used as holistic management concept (Hyperspace 2010; Value Competence Consulting 2002; Bodmer and Völker 2000). Moreover, the BSC should not be used as an additional top-down controlling instrument as this would only cause extra efforts and an additional reporting line (McCunn 1998).

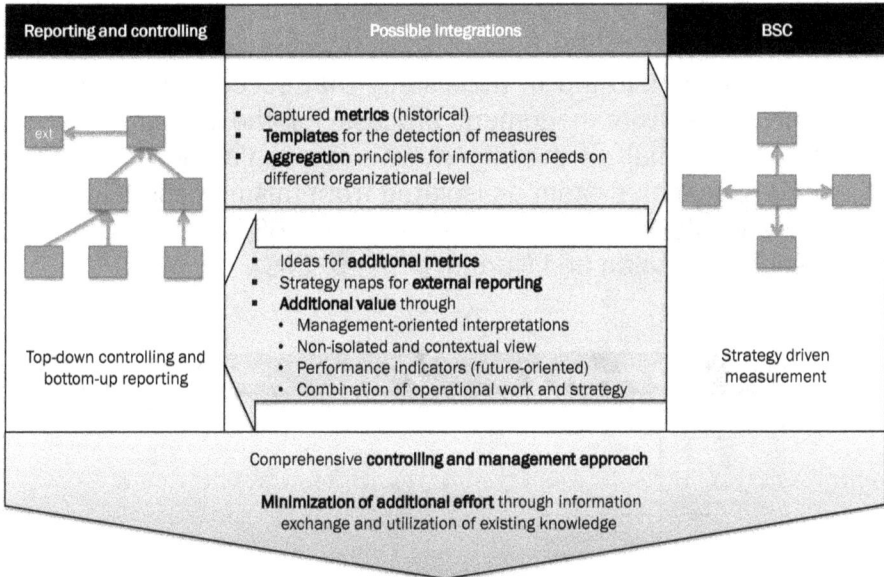

Figure 13: Integration of a BSC in a controlling and reporting system
[Source: own illustration]

Figure 13 summarizes knowledge and information flows between controlling and reporting on the one side and the BSC on the other side: It becomes evident that line reporting can contribute especially facts and approaches to create and abstract information as well as historical data to create targets in the organization. The BSC, on the other hand, can in return provide additional knowledge as it is a management concept. A combination of both frameworks can reduce efforts and can implement a balanced system of management and controlling.

### Allocation Processes

The BSC needs to be combined with the planning and budgeting processes, because it depicts the priorities of a company (Ghosh and Mukherjee 2006). In this book, a more holistic view will be taken: The resource allocations in general and the associated processes have to be linked to the BSC as it defines operational actions and initiatives (Bodmer and Völker 2000; Schermann and Volcic 2009; Kaplan and Norton 1996; Bauer 2010). Kaplan and Norton (1997, pp. 247ff.) demonstrated in their study that successful companies use their strategic management process for the allocation of resources, despite half of the interviewed companies described their particular allocation system as isolated from this process. Figure 14 shows a **step down approach** that uses the BSC to overcome the gap described (Kaplan and Norton 1997, p. 249).

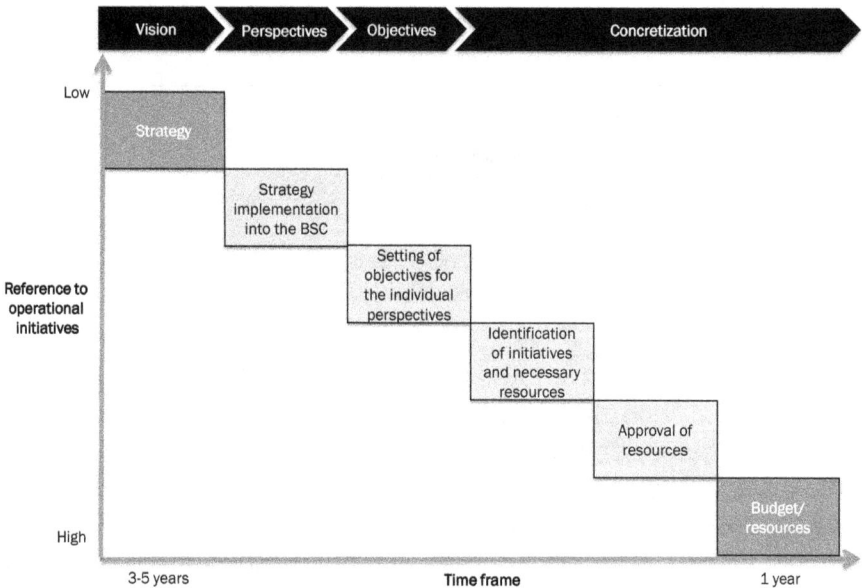

Figure 14: Step down approach for the usage of BSC in the allocation process
[Source: own illustration, adopted from Kaplan and Norton (1997, p. 249)]

In addition, enough resources (especially time and budget) need to be available for all participating sections during the application of a BSC (Hyperspace 2010; Pandey 2005). This is an important aspect as the expenses for the operation of the BSC approach are often underestimated in business practice (McCunn 1998).

### Risk Management

In many publications, a combination of the BSC with risk management can be found. The type of integration ranges between mere additional documentation, creation of a new perspective and the detailed documentation of risks and opportunities for individual strategic objectives or initiatives. The third and most intensive type of integration is recommended in management literature specialized on risk management and BSC topics. All these aspects influence the target path of measures accordingly.

## 4.2.4 Advantages

Full integration of the BSC with the described components can generate the following key benefits:

- By considering other organizational frameworks, the BSC will avoid biased planning and can be used as an extensive management tool (Ghosh and Mukherjee 2006). Moreover, the integrated approach can prevent an isolated reflection of only single aspects (Hyperspace 2010) and thus supports the idea of a comprehensive and company-wide management system.
- The combination with incentive schemes is particularly important as employees have to support the usage of the BSC in their daily business (Blackall 2007; Angel and Rampersad 2005). With the help of an incentive system, it becomes clearer how the operations in the processes and the contribution of each employee contribute to the overall success (Peters 2008). Bauer (2010) mentions that this integration can generate the accountability necessary for reaching the respective objectives on all organizational levels.

- Integration in the allocation process can foster acceptance and support of the entire system by linking resources to the importance of initiatives (Kaplan and Norton 1997, pp. 247ff.).
- The use of IT and automation can result in time and cost advantages (Blackall 2007) and provides additional transparency (Bauer 2010). Saving of resources can again increase the acceptance of the BSC.

### 4.2.5 Limitations and Restrictions

Since only existing management frameworks can be integrated, the ingredient is, of course, limited to them. When there are no concepts as IT support or incentive systems in place, they cannot be integrated. In this case it is up to the management to decide whether such systems should rather be implemented in order to profit from synergies (see also ingredient 1, *Introduction and Plannung*).

The ratio of the added burden compared to the extra benefits that result from a combination also restricts the integration with other concepts. While additional expenses can be easily measured quantitatively (for example by hours spent, implementation costs for the IT system, costs for additional incentives), the determination of the additional benefit is a more complex task. There is evidence that the BSC should not be turned into a second controlling instrument (McCunn 1998) and that administration should not exxagerate (Bauer 2010).

### 4.2.6 Introduction

The implementation strategy for this ingredient highly depends on the realization of already established aspects and their maturity within the management system in a company.

| | Component is available | Component is not (yet) available |
|---|---|---|
| **Strategy process** | Note and promote mutual influence | Usage of the BSC approach as initial form of strategy process |
| **IT support** | Check if a professional IT tool is required and force automation | Depending on knowledge and need implementation of standard software to support reporting and analyses |
| **Incentive system** | Link existing award payments in whole or in part to the achievement of objectives of the BSC (extrinsic motivation) | Assist for effective usage (intrinsic motivation) and introduction a combined incentive system |
| **Controlling and reporting** | Clarify information flows and connection in order to create synergies and reduce efforts | No explicit implications |
| **Allocation processes** | Consideration of the BSC | Usage of the BSC as initial allocation guideline |

Figure 15: Introductory implications for the integration of a BSC
[Source: own illustration]

Figure 15 summarizes best practices depending on whether the respective component is already established (available) or not. If a concept or framework already exists, the BSC needs to be integrated. If a component is not (yet) available, this figure shows if the introduction of this component together with the BSC is reasonable or even necessary for success.

## 4.2.7 Example of Application

### Corporate Level

After the introduction and implementation of the BSC at the corporate level, the concept needed to be integrated in a variety of already existing corporate frameworks.

#### Strategy Process

It was possible to describe four essential company units or areas playing an important role in the corporate strategy process of ABC. Their interactions and responsibilities in the BSC strategy process are shown in table 4: While the management board is primarily responsible for communicating the mission and strategy, the senior management committee analyzes and controls the implementation of initiatives. The departments are mainly in charge of planning and implementing the strategy.

Table 2: Integration of the BSC on corporate level with the strategy process

| Level | Description | Focus in the strategy process | Operational actions |
|---|---|---|---|
| Management Board | Important decisions, especially those involving large volumes, are made by the top management of ABC. This level can use the BSC as tool for the strategy review and as a communication medium. | ▪ Mission<br>▪ Controlling | ▪ Responsibility for the corporate BSC (including possibility of delegation)<br>▪ Quarterly review of the strategy implementation<br>▪ Act as a promoter of the corporate strategy<br>▪ Annual communication of corporate strategy with the help of the BSC |
| Steering committee | The steering committee of ABC is a regular meeting of top executives (including the heads of business groups and the management board). In this committee, all business areas present their current activities. | ▪ Mission<br>▪ Analysis<br>▪ Controlling | ▪ Top management should explain strategy to top executives to pave the way for cascading<br>▪ Critical reflection of the corporate BSC one a year to establish the strategies and strategic objectives<br>▪ All business groups and departments should present their BSC at each meeting |
| Departments | Since the individual business groups operate very independently, the actual strategy of ABC is the sum of these sub-strategies implemented and operated in the departments. This is viewed critically, as many projects and activities at the level of the business areas do not appear explicitly within the overall strategy. | ▪ Analysis<br>▪ Planning<br>▪ Implementation | ▪ Instead of adapting the strategy subsequently, the BSC realizes the corporate base for all operations<br>▪ The corporate BSC is cascaded in the departments<br>▪ The business group or functional areas implement the strategy at an operational level |

[Source: own illustration]

*Information Technology*

Since no dedicated IT support for a BSC was in use, existing IT systems of the company should be used to support the BSC. This decision could also further promote acceptance by employees because no additional IT training was needed in the first step.

Thus the software solutions should include:

- **Microsoft SharePoint Services:** ABC used the document management system Microsoft SharePoint (SharePoint) in many departments and processes to create, manage and share documents, forms and reports. SharePoint could therefore be used as an administrative system for BSC documents.
- **Microsoft Excel: Excel** was widely used within ABC for reporting, planning and calculation purposes. In particular, office workers and professional users were very familiar with this software. Thus **Excel** was used for data entry.

All participating processes got individual SharePoint workspaces that were fully configured. Forms were deployed and provided in a folder tree structure (see appendix). In the process workspaces, employees could organize forms and documents that were necessary for the operation of the cascaded BSC. Those in charge of the BSC held adminstration rights.

Currently great efforts have been made within ABC to introduce the ARIS platform for the documentation of business processes. Once the ARIS-based documentation has been completed for most processes and the live operation of the BSC have stabilized, the strategy management team will evaluate if the integration of ARIS BSC can enrich or substitute the available SharePoint solution.

*Incentive System*

According to this ingredient the BSC needs to be integrated into the existing incentive systems. ABC already has a two-part incentive system, consisting of the two following components:

- **Synergy goals**: The achievement of these financial goals depends on the performance of the respective unit or the performance of the ABC group at all. These goals cannot be directly influenced by an individual employee and realize 30% of the variable income. The idea behind this goal is that the support of all employees will contribute to the overall success of the processes and will thus influence the performance of the complete organization.
- **Commitment goals**: These committed goals can directly be influenced by the employee and are agreed individually with the manager.

The commitment goals are documented annually in a target agreement form. Appendix A.7 provides a new and modified target agreement form based on the previous form currently in use at ABC but including the specific references to the BSC.

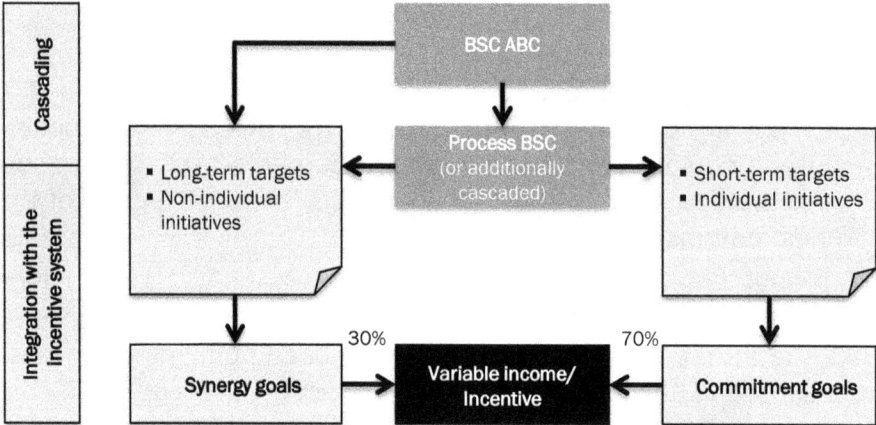

Figure 16: Cascading and integration with the existing incentive system
[Source: own illustration]

The BSC of a process and the corporate BSC may include several objectives and initiatives that can become part of the incentive system.

The goals and initiatives of the BSC, which can be directly related to individual employees, are included in the commitment goals. As shown in figure 26, thus the short-term goals influence 70% of the variable income of employees. The other 30% will be determined by community work and long-term goals, which are documented at the process or corporate level. The corporate goals are presented and discussed at the BSC workshop at the beginning of each year.

*Controlling and Reporting*

As already described, the controlling and reporting function within ABC is highly dependent on the participating processes and in particular on the respective reporting line. Therefore, the formulation of general rules for integration with the existing reporting becomes quite difficult.

The BSC was thus introduced as a management concept independent from the available reporting system. The process responsibles should understand that the BSC is a tool for strategically organizing business activities.

In total, as described in ingredient 2, some starting points for the combination and integration of both systems was introduced on a step-by-step basis. It was for example encouraged that the process owners present their business activities based on the BSC in multiple channels such as the intranet or in the senior management committee. Moreover, for example, the existing reporting strategies, which were often available within departments and processes, were gradually adapted to the objectives of the BSC and by doing so, the objectives of the reporting organizational units became clearer and more transparent in the whole organization.

*Allocation Process*

From the former organizationzal setting, it could be concluded that the distribution of budget and resources for central departments and business groups within ABC are often not organized in a transparent manner. Some employees explicitly call for more accountability in the allocation of resources within the company. For this reason, the departments and processes submit their budget and resource planning by relying on the contents of the corporate BSC (e. g. based on the initiative map) and top management can provide the resources according to the corporate BSC. In this manner ABC can benefit from two main advantages: First, the distribution of resources and budget becomes more transparent and secondly, strategy-oriented resource allocation is aligned with the company vision.

*Risk Management*

Risk management aspects play a very important role for ABC due to the kind of business, the risk potential of their facilities, and the materials used in the chemical industry, so this integration is also vital for the success of the BSC. On the one hand, this fact is partly a consequence of the company's political and social environment. On the other hand, security aspects of the chemical technology force the explicit consideration of risks.

The internal requirements were specified in the risk management department so that issues of risk management can be considered in the BSC approach. Risks are defined as potential negative target deviations, whose occurrence triggers appropriate and planned countermeasures (PWC n.d.).

In an extensive analysis on the integration of risk management (Peters 2008) two fundamental results were documented: First, the original BSC does not support risk management very well. Second, a hybrid integration of a performance-based BSC should be introduced to support risk management most efficiently. Considering these two recommendations, risks are recognized for the overall BSC system as well as for planned initiatives.

For the implementation at ABC, two documents (appendix A.11) were launched for integrating risk management:

- **Structural risks:** These kinds of risks apply to the entire organization (or process) and can be both endogenous as well as exogenous. Endogenous risks are predominately within the decision-making power of the company (e. g. protection against theft of delivery goods) while exogenous risks are completely outside of the company's control (e. g. new tax laws).

- **Action-based risks:** These operational and strategic risks arise directly from the actions of the company. In the case of integration with the BSC, these risks on target achievements result from planned initiatives at the operational or strategic level.

For both types of risks, prevention strategies and countermeasures for the consideration of the risk events are documented. In addition, the impact of the occurrence of the risks on target achievement needs to be estimated (appendix A.11).

The detailed survey on risks (preventive actions, responsive actions) was conducted in a separate risk workshop after the third BSC workshop (see ingredient 1) or after the second improvement workshop (see ingredient 6). However, the description of the risks as well as the estimation of impacts on target achievement should be directly included in the BSC workshops, because the internal guidelines of ABC recommend describing risks at the same time as strategy decisions are made. It should also be noted that in many internal business areas, risk catalogs are already available within ABC. In this case, these documented risks should also be used as starting point for the BSC.

With the described procedure, a truly realistic picture of the strategy will be developed and risk management becomes an integral part of the operational and strategic business of ABC.

### Process Level

The BSC were integrated in the existing framework of the logistics processes after their implementation.

It was of particular note in this case that the BSC was used as an opportunity in the logistic process to introduce much-needed IT systems for the next years. The respective department has urgently analyzed the long-postponed goal to remove several business process interfaces. These initiatives are now documented in the personal BSCs.

### Strategy Process

In the logistic process, no explicit strategy process had been organized so far, and team meetings mainly discussed short-term as well as operational activity-based issues. Thus, during the BSC introduction workshops, the process team had to run through a complete strategy process and also discussed long-term as well as fundamental new business goals. Employees recognized that many legacy structures have been accepted so far. This provided them with the opportunity to critically reflect these structures (e. g. the handling of customs issues without a corresponding process definition) and trigger new optimization initiatives (e. g. definition of a process customs issues).

### IT Support

The logistics process did not use SharePoint for internal coordination. In the pilot project the currently implemented solutions (a proprietary logistics portal) was used in order to guarantee a smooth BSC introduction. All forms and documents, which can be found in the appendix of this book, were filled out with Microsoft Word and Microsoft EXCEL. The implementation of SharePoint was specified and will be performed in the second year of the BSC application.

### Incentive System

To achieve a learning effect through learning by doing, it is recommended not to fully integrate the BSC within the incentive system during the first year. Instead, the personal BSCs should be provided parallel to the known target agreements. However, this target agreement can include a limited number of **real initiatives** from the developed BSCs.

This combination was intensified for the logistic process, as the employees have been familiar with this type of target agreements based on strategy workshops of the previous years.

### Controlling and Reporting

Until the enterprise-wide rollout of the BSC, all documents (e. g. the strategy map) were used predominantly for internal communication within the departments and processes, as other, major parts of the organization needed explanations of the BSC concept first. However, the process owners could use the documents for presentations to top management (for example in the next meeting of the senior management committee) and thus contributed to a positive image of the BSC.

After the company-wide implementation of the BSC, the presented controlling and reporting system was used.

### Allocation Process

The results (strategy map and objectives with the documented measures) were presented to the process owners in order to gain the approval for further actions and measurement. These results were taken into account within the allocating process for the re-sources for the next year. For example, the logistic process owner should, according to the strategy map, assign more employees to the areas of supplier management, the reduction of IT interfaces and the definition of procedures to realize an efficient long-term business instead of focusing only on the short-term activities of daily work.

### Risk Management

The documentation of risks (including the risk workshop), was not executed in the first year of the pilot application, but was performed in the second year of BSC usage. This was due to the fact that this would have further increased the complexity of the new concept. This would have perhaps also led to negative reactions by the em-ployees. Moreover employees had not to face negative conse-quences for non-achievement of the objectives (see incentive sys-tem) in the first year anyway.

## 4.3    Ingredient 3: Cascading

| For the quick reader | |
| --- | --- |
| **Fundamental spice** | "Cascading of the Balanced Scorecard is the key to success.", Niven 2009 |
| **Ingredient 3 in a nutshell** | A BSC cannot exist, if it is separated from existing strategy processes, incentive systems, controlling and reporting activities as well as from allocation and risk management processes. A successful BSC needs to go along with existing frameworks but can of course influence and change the existing systems. |

### *4.3.1 Definition*

The concept of **cascading** has found its way into diverse sectors, such as programming languages (Meyer 2007, p. 68), optical communication technology (Schunk, Bahl and Unrau 2002, p. 737) or the usage of fuel cells (Winkler 2002, p. 374 ).

In business and management practice this term generally describes the need for specific actions at the lower levels of an organization based on overall targets. An alignment of individual tasks (e.g., in the departments) with the mission of the organization makes the overall goals visible and feasible for employees (Edinger 2009, pp. 236f.).

### *4.3.2 Background*

Unlike the rollout of the BSC (see ingredient 1, *Planning and Introduction*) which is the horizontal implementation of the BSC in an organization, cascading means breaking down and operationalizing a BSC at process, team or individual level (Hendricks, Menor and Wiedmann 2004). This approach is illustrated in figure 17.

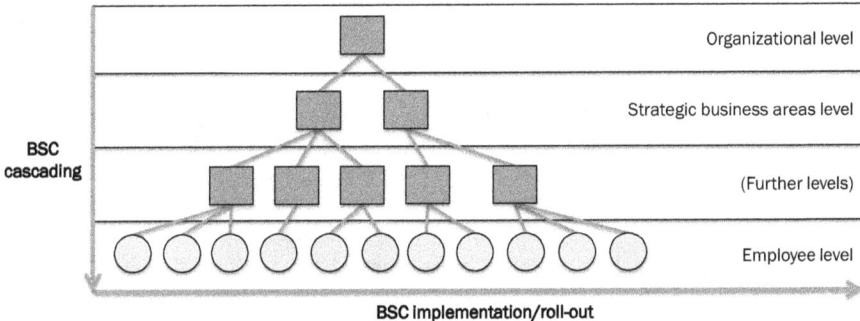

Figure 17: Cascading as vertical spread of strategic objectives within an organization
[Source: own illustration, adopted from Kaplan and Norton (2001)]

A company which uses the BSC as performance management approach should implement the BSC as a central starting point of all business activities (Schermann and Volcic 2009). The lack of sufficient cascading of the BSC to lower levels is one of the key reasons for the failure of the whole concept (Niven 2002). Beginning with a clear vision and strategy (Richardson 2004), the contents of the BSC (strategic objectives, performance measures, and targets) should be implemented in departments or low-level business processes and be used in daily business (McCunn 1998; Kaplan and Norton 2001; Schermann and Volcic 2009). A meaningful cascading, including a consistent target system, is a key success factor to bring the BSC to life (Kaplan and Norton 2001).

## 4.3.3 Components

This ingredient will look at the **strategy break down** in a narrow sense (pure transfer of targets into smaller units with shorter time horizont) as well as at related conditions (**Priority of strategy** and

**Strategy Reference**), which support the cascading idea in a broader sense. Figure 18 summarizes this view.

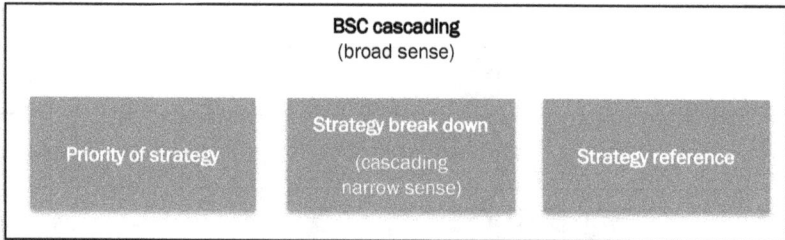

Figure 18: Components of BSC cascading
[Source: own illustration]

### Priority of Strategy

The component of cascading describes that first of all, the map of vision, mission and strategy of a company definitely needs to be communicated before cascading (Bauer 2010). The implementation of the BSC at various organizational levels must thus be driven by a set of strategic objectives (Richardson 2004; Peters 2008; Bodmer and Völker 2000). The breaking down can only be successful if the units of the cascading are in line with a corporate strategy (Hyperspace 2010; Kaplan and Norton 2001; Angel and Rampersad 2005; Richardson 2004). Conversely, the lack of strategy is a prominent mistake that often leads to the failure of the approach (Niven 2002).

### Strategy Break Down

The breaking down process is the cascading approach in a narrow sense: Beginning at an appropriate level (like the top level of an organization), a BSC is designed. Afterwards, subordinate units provide their own BSCs (Schermann and Volcic 2009), in which they describe how they want to achieve the superordinate objectives (Pandey 2005). The supportive character is important during breaking down processes to lower levels of processes, divisions and teams (Hendricks, Menor and Wiedmann 2004). Cascading in the narrow sense should not be used for additional top-down control

(McCunn 1998). In contrary, the aim of cascading is that every employee gets the opportunity to contribute to the overall vision and strategy (Kaplan and Norton 1996) and that each employee is aware of his or her contribution (Bauer 2010).

The question which level is most suitable for the implementation of the highest scorecard is much-discussed in case studies: While a launch on the overall organizational level of the company is most probably widespread, also higher levels such as cross-organizational supply chains can serve as parent instance (Reichert 2006). Other guidelines state the level of organizational departments or functional divisions as an appropriate starting point. This approach, however, can only realize limited and isolated optimization.

Different opinions and experiences are known concerning the question of the last cascading level: While sometimes departments and processes can serve as the final BSC instance the original idea of the concept was to "make strategy everyone's job" (Kaplan and Norton 2001; Schermann and Volcic 2009). This leads to individual employees, who have personal BSCs on the last level of cascading (Niven 2009, p. 239).

### Strategy Reference

The first component of the ingredient (priority of strategy) requires that the strategy is set up before the actual cascading can start. The second component (strategy break down) summarizes key rules for a vertical break down in a company. This third component calls for a precise causal relationship in between these two areas.

In a first step, the contents of the cascaded BSCs must take into account the specific characteristics of the overall strategy (Schermann and Volcic 2009). This means that strategic objectives and actions which do not match the superordinate BSC should be excluded (Mair 2002).

Second, it is important that the activities can be traced. The BSC should be cascaded into the organization so all employees can clearly identify their contribution to the achievement of the strategic corporate objectives (Bauer 2010). An important aim is to clearly emphasize the cause-and-effect relation between individual performance and overall success (Othman et al. 2006). Sometimes it can be recommended to present cause-effect diagrams to employees (Hyperspace 2010) to motivate strategy-oriented acting. It can be recommended as a guideline that all activities should be reviewed in terms of their contribution to the overall corporate strategy (Peters 2008).

## 4.3.4 Advantages

The usage of this ingredient helps to avoid the problem that initiatives and actions appear isolated and are not understood in a comprehensive context (Hyperspace 2010). Each unit should have the opportunity to clearly grasp its share in the overall company business (Bauer 2010). Employees can actively determine how they reach goals, which is an essential requirement of the BSC (Peters 2008). In addition, the cascading process leads to logical and transparent derivatives, which helps to explain its impact on individual employees (PricewaterhouseCoopers n.d.). Cascading renders the BSC application in a company-wide rollout transparent and traceable. Moreover, all activities in the organizations can be brought in line and thus isolated optimizations (for example in only one single team) are avoided. Cascading implementation at all levels of an organization maximizes the success of the entire BSC concept (Richardson 2004).

## 4.3.5 Limitations and Restrictions

The level of granularity of the cascading process becomes critical at the end of the cascading line. The extra efforts of an additional break down (involving, for example, time for workshops, or efforts to document the new BSC) must be evaluated in relation to the benefits offered. In small teams, for instance, a task can just as well be directly assigned, without the need to create a further BSC at the level of that team.

A possible solution is the idea to stop cascading as soon as the target of the initiative (recognizable by its focus on **what** is to be achieved) drifts off and turns into merely operational instructions for the implementation of initiatives (focus shifting to **how** something is to be achieved).

## 4.3.6 Introduction

At the pilot project stage (see ingredient 1, *Planning and Introduction*), i. e., at the beginning of launching the BSC, the cascading process can obviously only be put into practice to a very limited extent. Since the pilot project will be implemented only in a clearly outlined and thus also limited part of the organization (in most cases only one department or division), no parent BSC will be available at that time. However it is recommended to cascade to a meaningful level of detail as early as possible (team or employee level, for example).

From the start of the corporate BSC onwards, strategic objectives should be cascaded to ensure that the system will not degenerate into short-term reporting structures, but will allow clear strategy references to be drawn from the top of the company to the level of BSC for each employee. Only by following this cascading structure, the strategy of the top management can be operationally implemented. Furthermore, a fully developed cascading structure can create synergies and additional benefits (such as the integration of an incentive system).

## 4.3.7 Example of Application

### Corporate Level

*Priority of Strategy*

As shown in figure 27, the vision and strategy of ABC was clarified before the cascading process was scheduled. This orientation to the overall company strategy was also supported by a time-delayed approach: Since the corporate BSC was first introduced and the departments or business processes owners have been strongly involved, the vision and the strategic objectives of ABC were made clear before cascading. Moreover the strategic objectives of the initiative map were binding documents for the departments.

### Strategy Break Down

The implementation process and the process of continuous improvement, which were already present at the corporate level, could have also been used in the processes of ABC. However, the following changes were necessary:

- **Participants:** The person in charge of the process mainly led the BSC workshops. He or she had the overall responsibility for the project.
- **Kick-off:** The kick-off was only necessary when the process teams create the BSC for the first time. Instead of the top managers, all or parts of the departmental workforce should participate.
- **Workshops:** Depending on the number of employees, qualification of staff, and budget requirements, all process team members or a limited group of people participated in the workshops. For the selection of participants it was important to ensure that the team achieves an adequate cross-functional character and all major tasks of the department were included. In any case, the results of the workshop needed to be available to all employees in an appropriate form (e. g. strategy maps with explaining notes which can guarantee that employees understand the BSC).

These proposals are located between the two extreme forms of cascading (Horvath & Partners 2004, p. 244): On the one hand, the corporate BSC is not only a non-binding communication medium for the processes (this state would partly reflect the current procedure within ABC's reporting and strategy rollout). On the other hand, the corporate BSC is not entirely provided in a top-down fashion by top management. Rather, the BSC for a process is developed through a combination of mandatory joint initiatives (resulting from the initiative map), the vision of ABC as well as the vision of the processes.

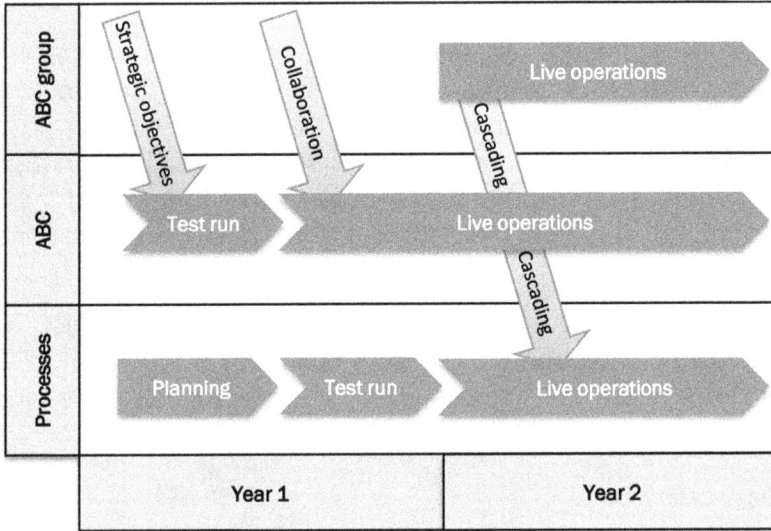

Figure 19: Comprehensive cascading
[Source: own illustration]

Another important aspect that must be considered in the strategy break-down is that the corporate BSC of ABC is in fact not reflecting the top level strategy. ABC is the regional company of the international ABC group (holding company with a widespread portfolio financing different industrial companies) and aligns its vision and strategy to the requirements of the group. Since the global launch required extensive political and corporate bridges, a step-by-step approach was used to convince the whole ABC group of the BSC concept (see figure 27):

- **Strategic objectives:** In the first step the expectation of the ABC group was only loosely connected to the corporate strategy map. In this case, the objectives of the Irish ABC group were included within the existing perspective.

- **Participation in workshops BSC (collaboration)**: In a second step, employees at the Irish headquarters were invited to participate in reviews and improvement workshops during the second year. In this way, the international colleagues better understood the benefits of the concept.
- **Group scorecard (cascading)**: However, the ultimate aim should be that in an ideal case, the Irish ABC group develops a scorecard at the highest level. In this case, the corporate BSC of ABC in Austria is already the first cascaded BSC. In general it should be recommended that an active formal and informal exchange process take place between the organizations, in order to strengthen the cooperative work aspect.

If this plan is implemented as described, the BSCs of ABC will finally be fullly cascaded. All individual initiatives of personal BSCs at the individual level will then be a result of the vision of the international ABC group.

*Strategy Reference*

Employees must be aware about their personal contribution to the company's strategy. Thus it made sense to give the employees a personal and an individual scorecard that could be used as a template for their daily work activities. As the target agreement forms are available within the SharePoint system, an integrated program can automatically generate personal BSCs based on this data.

Appendix A.8 shows how such a personal scorecard can look like. In particular the following aspects were important in order to achieve effective strategy referencing. They are already part of the suggested personal BSC form:

- **Graphical representation**: The perspectives as well as their dependencies are illustrated graphically.
- **Vision**: The visions of ABC and the vision of the processes appear on the top of the personal BSC. By linking individual goals with these visions, the employee's contribution to the enterprise value is illustrated.

- **Simplicity:** The personal BSC should become a template for daily work activities. Minimum and maximum values, risk management strategies and other complex information are released.

### Process Level

In the case of the logistic processes, the BSCs were of course created solely based on the developed visions of this process group, as they are realized as a pilot project. At this point, no corporate BSC was available. The process BSC reflects the overall strategy and is not directly influenced by a parent BSC.

However, it was noted several times in the pilot processes that some strategic objectives could not be effectively realized in an isolated process. For example, all internal customers (other departments which require logistics services) had to support the efficient data flow of logistic orders as well in order to ensure that data was correctly recorded and documented. This strategic goal could of course have been supported training and checklists, but it would be more efficient to have several process steps affirm the commitment to this objective in such a cross-functional process. The clear experience was made to focus pilot projects on processes instead of limiting the implementation on single departments. This requirement was in line with the idea of a process-oriented organization, where strategies are first implemented in processes. In a second step, the involved departments (organizational hierarchy) were addressed. In a nutshell, the process team welcomed the expansion of the BSC in the whole organization of ABC in the second year.

In the following year, the next step of cascading was performed and individual targets from the corporate scorecard were transferred to the process scorecard. Transferred goals were either linked directly or enriched by a more granular focus including details for the specific process.

The developed BSC (appendix A.14) have been reviewed and were cascaded to the next lower level (employee or team level). In the third workshop, the responsible process team members documented the responsibilities for each initiative in the formsheets (appendix A.14) and the personal BSCs for the employees in the process teams (see appendix A.8 for an example of a personal BSC).

## 4.4    Ingredient 4: Measurement

| For the quick reader | |
| --- | --- |
| **Fundamental spice** | "The development of the performance measures is a challenge.", Harber 1998 |
| **Ingredient 4 in a nutshell** | The suitable selection and development of indicators is one of the crucial points for a successful BSC. This ingredient describes compulsory (e.g. strategy-oriented, measurability, comprehensiveness) as well as balanced (e.g. many vs. view; hard vs. soft; early vs. late) aspects of good measures which leads to balanced performance management system. |

### 4.4.1 Definition

The correct choice, balance and consistency of indicators are particularly important aspects within the BSC. This ingredient intends to provide guidelines for establishing of an appropriate set of indicators.

### 4.4.2 Background

It is the selection of indicators that operationalizes strategy and targets when applying the BSC approach. To date, many guidelines have documented the requirements for an effective selection of indicators only in a very fragmentary and incomplete way. However, using correct measures can make an important contribution to ensuring that all necessary and important factors are considered and to achieving the necessary **balance** within the BSC.

Although essential for the BSC success (Peters 2008), the selection of indicators is especially challenging and requires continual work (Harber 1998).

### 4.4.3 Components

This ingredient compiles the requirements that will realize a good set of metrics. This kind of compilation of successful characteristics of indicators has not been documented in this holistic approach so far.

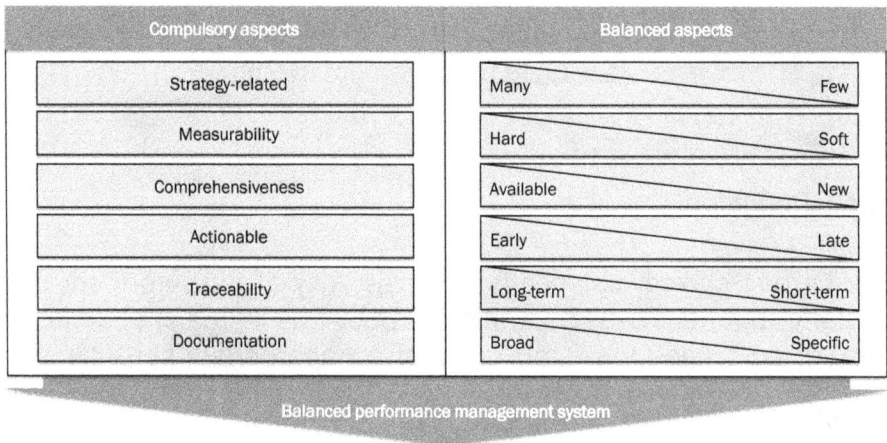

Figure 20: Compulsory and balanced aspects for indicators
[Source: own illustration]

There are two types of best practices regarding characteristics of measures: On the one hand, there are claims that should be followed in any case and their compliance is required. As these sub-components are binding and not negotiable in order to achieve a good BSC, these are called **compulsory**. On the other hand, there are factors that must be weighed on a continuum. They must be balanced in a manner that they provide a sane relationship between two extremes. These aspects are described as **balanced** in this ingredient.

### Compulsory Aspects

A general requirement is that all measures must always **be strategy-related**. This means that indicators must be in line with the strategic objectives of the BSC (Umbeck, Lederer and Nitze 2009, p. 393). Methods to secure this target can be found in ingredient 3 (chapter 4.3). All figures must be **measurable** (Pandey 2005) in order to refine targets and measure targetfulfillment (Bodmer and Völker 2000). Another advantage of this compulsory requirement is that only measurable quantities can be monitored meaningfully and thus allow changes to become observable (Angel and Rampersad 2005). Moreover, all indicators must be **actionable**, which means employees must be able to influence them with specific actions and initiatives (Bodmer and Völker 2000). When this requirement is met, endogenous parameters (like market growth) can be completely excluded and the operationalization of measures has priority (Umbeck, Lederer and Nitze 2009, p. 393). Indicators must be defined clearly, their definition and importance need to be **comprehensible**, and their meaning must be fully captured. A common language offers an important benefit (Peters 2008). **Traceability** is a further requirement: The BSC does not merely consist of a collection of existing, isolated figures, which are grouped into perspectives such as **business processes** and **customer**. If this really is the case, nearly all controlling instruments in companies would already constitute a BSC (Horvath & Partners 2007, p. 59). However, measures combined in the BSC create a coherent overall picture that can be traced, even in their relation to the major strategy (Hyperspace 2010). All these aspects imply that indicators should be **documented** comprehensively and that the types of documentation support the other aspects mentioned.

### Balanced Aspects

Typically the question about the correct number of measures arises: While there are only **few** figures that do not have sufficient explanatory power, the identification and analysis of too **many** indicators will, on the other hand, take too much effort and will therefore harm the overall concept as well as the organization (Angel and Rampersad 2005). Based on a specific study, Kaplan and Norton (2001, p. 330) suggest that each scorecard should employ 20-25 indicators, which are evenly distributed over all perspectives.

A fundamental point, in which the BSC differs from other known controlling models, is that soft factors and soft (often also called non-financial or non-monetary) metrics are explicitly included (Angel and Rampersad 2005; Othman et al. 2006; Horvath & Partners 2007, p. 60; Horvath and Kaufmann 1998, p. 9). A company's success and therefore necessarily the entire management system should be based upon the management of financial as well as non-financial measures which cannot be measured or weighed numerically (Horvath & Partners 2007, pp. 64ff.). Thus, a successful company should also rather focus on soft indicators such as customer or employee satisfaction (Horvath & Partners 2007, pp. 64ff.). **Hard** and **soft** metrics have the same, balanced importance within the BSC (Horvath & Partners 2007, p. 60). A non-financial share of even up to 80% might be acceptable in some cases (Kaplan and Norton 2001, p. 330). However, measuring soft factors on the basis of a scale is often vague and open to criticism, of course (Horvath & Partners 2007, pp. 204ff.). Nevertheless, measurable figures remain a compulsory feature (Pandey 2005). Another important aspect seems to be that during the ongoing operation of the BSC, a company will need to counteract the typical trend of financial ratios gradually replacing non-monetary ones (Eilers 2005, p. 5; Horvath and Kaufmann 1998, p. 9).

Another requirement for balance refers to the ratio of known (**available**), previously established and **new**, still to be developed indicators. While some guidelines clearly recommend that the BSC should contain a certain proportion of new figures never recorded before (Niven 2002), other management handbooks state major concerns about new measures due to the additional costs for collecting and documenting these indicators (Value Competence Consulting 2002). Since the BSC is neither a replacement nor a second line of basic reporting or controlling (Bauer 2010), it seems reasonable to ensure for a balanced mix of new and old metrics. Nevertheless, old indicators should only be used if those previously set standards still fit exactly into the new framework of the BSC (Umbeck, Lederer and Nitze 2009, p. 393) and only if they specifically measure strategy achievement. As the selection of measures included needs to be checked constantly and regularly, it may occur that new indicators become necessary and older figures can be excluded (Harber 1998).

The time horizon is also a fundamental and mission-critical aspect. Although the indicators of the BSC are aimed at supporting daily work (Williams 2004), they should also allow a **long-term** supply and long-term performance measurement (Hendricks, Menor and Wiedmann 2004). As a consequence, the selection of indicators should focus on a healthy mix of leading and lagging indicators. Additionally, the exact configuration of this mix may depend on the hierarchy level of the BSC, because BSCs on staff-level, for example, require a **short-term** combination with an incentive system.

Moreover, measures must be balanced between generic, **broad** indicators and very **specific** measures. BSCs more towards the top of the cascading line will contain broader indicators (e. g. aggregated turnover) which cover a variety of different business situations (e. g. individual turnover results of different business areas).

### 4.4.4 Advantages

The advantages of this ingredient are already reflected in the individual components of the term **BSC**:

- **Balanced**: The balanced aspects ensure that the strategy will be measured in a balanced way. Unlike other well-known management and controlling concepts, not only historic and short-term statements about a business are made - the BSC is also looking into the future.
- **Score**: Choosing the right indicators is critical to the overall success of the BSC. Even if the above-mentioned compulsory aspects are considered, the BSC will not degenerate into a

mere reporting tool as the measures rather reflect strategy achievement. Thus, the vision of a company becomes measurable.

- **Card**: The measurement by a BSC takes the most important indicators into account and depicts the achievement of strategic goals. The term card, which reminds of sports (like a handy golf-course card), also implies that the economic status of the strategy can be clearly read and interpreted.

### 4.4.5 Limitations and Restrictions

The aspects categorized as **compulsory** describe requirements that need to be included without exception. It seems to be possible to reject these binding demands in very special and rare cases only. Compulsory requirements are extremely correlated to the overall success of the BSC.

As explained above, **balanced** aspects should aim a good balance. If the configuration of the organization requires tending towards one extreme but justifiable position, this consideration is also possible.

### 4.4.6 Introduction

As the definition and selection of measures is the critical phase in practice, the components of this ingredient focus primarily on the identification of adequate indicators. The development of targets and initiatives, however, is also part of the basic recipe (chapter 3). Figure 21 shows the process of refinement in detail, including the described components and further best practices in this area

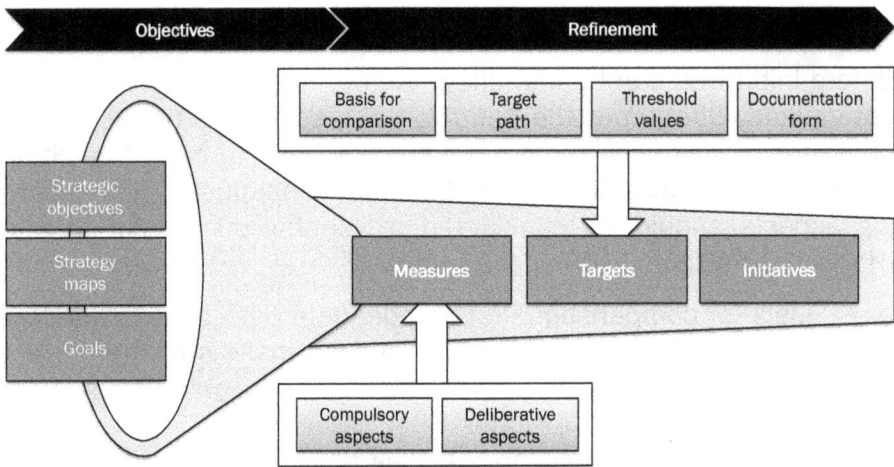

Figure 21: Introduction of the ingredient "measurement"
[Source: own illustration]

### Process Input

Goals and requirements of the BSC, strategic objectives within the perspectives and the visualization of these strategic objectives (with strategy maps, for example) are the input necessary for refinement (all resulting from ingredient 1).

### Measures

In the actual selection of indicators, both, the **compulsory** aspects as well as the **balanced** aspects have to be taken into account (Hendricks, Menor and Wiedmann 2004; Williams 2004). The following checklist questions are quite helpful (Horvath & Partners 2007, pp. 207f.):

- Is it possible to achieve the strategic objective by using this indicator?
- Is an unambiguous interpretation of the indicator possible?
- Can the employees influence the indicator?

Various methods can be used for the identification and selection, such as audits, workshops, staff meetings or instructions.

### Targets

Before initiatives can be identified, targets for measures should be determined. Oftentimes the definition of **lead targets** (What can we do better to stay ahead?) is more suitable than to record **catch-up targets** (What should be done to become competitive?). The following aspects should be considered to identify successful targets (Horvath & Partners 2007, pp. 214ff.):

- **Basis for comparison:** First an adequate data base is needed, whose sources can be benchmarking, analysis of the current state of the company, strategic objectives or customer surveys.
- **Target path:** The path to reaching the intended target should also be planned. A desired growth rate of 50% in five years does not automatically mean an increase of 10% per year. The acceleration of quick wins can rather increase the success rate in the first years. Or one-time investments could be necessary, which may reduce the success rate in the first years. In general, outlining the target paths for a timespan of about three to five years is recommended.
- **Threshold values:** Since achieving precise targets at an exact point in time is not plausible in general, thresholds should be set up. It would be best to integrate these thresholds with risk management (see ingredient 2).
- **Documentation form:** The final step is the documentation of the targets, including formal parameters and nominal values per year. Data sources and responsibilities should also be documented.

### Initiatives

For the development of necessary initiatives, it is recommended to apply creativity techniques like brainstorming as a first step. Moreover, a matrix can be used to visualize which initiatives support which strategic objectives. Strategic targets provide guidelines for resource allocation and prioritization of actions (Horvath & Partners 2007, p. 222 ff.)

## 4.4.7 Example of Application

### Corporate Level

According to ingredient 4, the compulsory aspects of good measures must be considered in any case when setting up a measurement system. Balanced aspects must be balanced between two extreme forms.

#### Compulsory Aspects

In the second BSC workshop, the strategy management presented and explained the compulsory aspects of good indicators with examples (positive and negative ones). The participants realized that these aspects are very important to be considered in the development of key measures in the small groups. Moreover, the compulsory requirements for good measures became part of the training concept **BSC expert** (see ingredient 5).

The consideration of most compulsory aspects is also supported by the different forms (see appendices A.5, A.7 and A.8) which can be used. For example, the documentation of indicators always features a graphical or logical reference to the strategic objective and to the vision. The obligatory mentioning of the data source for nominators and denominators can guarantee measurability; the recommended numbering structure and the reference fields can secure good traceability and adequate documentation. A clear understanding of the measures is supported by the explicit inclusion of a long description as well as a guideline on how to interpret the indicator.

Within the continuous process (see ingredient 6), it was also up to the strategy management to check that the compulsory aspects of the measures are considered in the improvement workshops.

#### Balanced Aspects

Based on the interview with the management board of ABC, it was possible to formulate fundamental guidelines for the indicators.

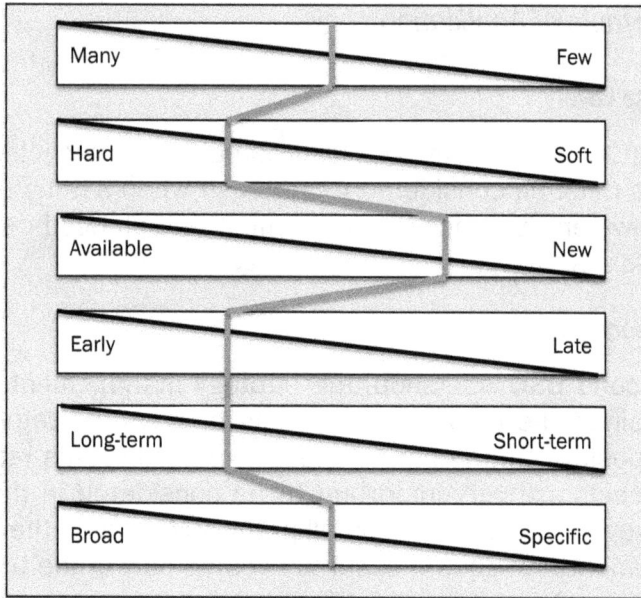

Figure 22: Top management expectations from BSC measures
[Source: own illustration]

The demands of ABC's top management were combined with the balanced aspects for BSC indicators. The results are shown in figure 28:

- Compared to the previous reports of ABC and its departments, the BSC should include fewer but more powerful measures for strategic interpretations. A balanced set of about 20 indicators was recommended.
- Even though the BSC should focus on soft and non-monetary factors, these seem to be inappropriate for the corporate scorecard. Soft measures are more suitable for inclusion in the cascaded scorecards (process or personal level).
- Frequently, known indicators did not allow for a profound statement about the strategy's success in the past. Therefore the measures of the corporate BSC were new and created according to vision and strategy of ABC.

- An explicit request of the management board was to focus more on early indicators because historical and short-term data is already a dominant part of the existing controlling and reporting systems.
- Indicators should mainly be of a long-term nature.
- There was no particular focus on specific or broad measures.

## Process Level

In case of the logistic processes, the strategy management team gave a short training session as part of the introduction workshops on how to develop good measures. In addition, the author presented typical measurement systems for logistics enterprises, which were very welcomed as motivation for own results.

### Balanced Aspects

In the kick-offs with the process team, the balanced aspects of ingredient 4 were discussed and documented. These decisions were made using a scale (see figure 23). This early assignment had the advantage that the requirements for measures were named without knowing the results from workshops and thus provide a non-biased picture of the goals.

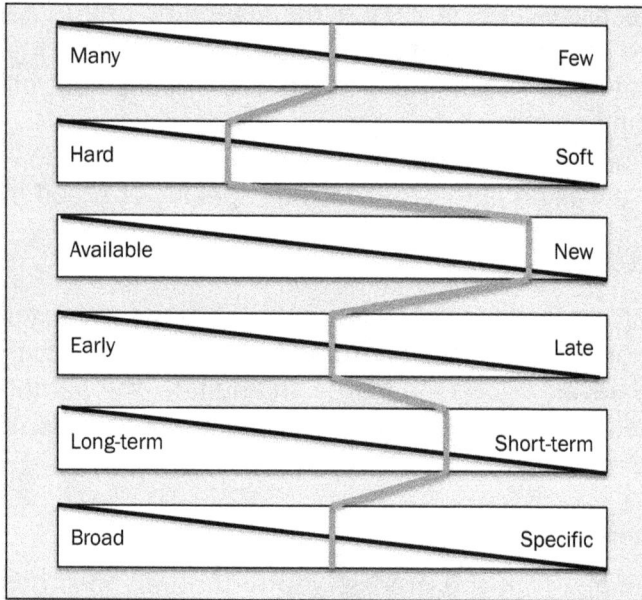

Figure 23: Requested balanced aspects for measures
[Source: own illustration]

After finishing the second workshop, the strategy management team investigated if the developed indicators actually met the desired balanced aspects. In the third workshops, proposals were discussed and some measures were changed in a way that the BSCs meet the balanced aspects. As a result of this approach the process BSCs were aligned with the ex-ante formulated focus.

*Compulsory Aspects*

Beside the balanced aspects, compulsory aspects must also be considered. The development of measures in workshops was actively accompanied by the strategy management team and by way of processing a checklist with mandatory measurement key questions[10], so the team could guarantee that all compulsory aspects were considered.

In the case of the logistic process, all measures were new and have been developed based on the strategy map.

The existing measures were fundamentally revised in the workshops. The majority of existing indicators has not been measured in recent years. In addition, most of the measures did not meet the mandatory aspects of ingredient 4. The form used to systematically document the strategic goals and indicators (appendix A.5 and A.6) has substantially contributed to the compulsory aspects (e. g. the documentation of data sources that was not previously recorded before). For some of the strategic objectives, no documented measures existed so far. For these cases the author supports the design of appropriate indicators.

---

10    The following example questions are an excerpt from the checklist: „Is it possible to conduct measurements with justifiable expenses?" for the aspect "measureable" or „Can the value of the measure be affected by the actions of the department or individual employees?" for the aspect "actionable".

## 4.5    Ingredient 5: Acceptance and Support

| For the quick reader | |
| --- | --- |
| **Fundamental spice** | "Everyone must be gradually introduced to the new concept." PricewaterhouseCoopers n.d. |
| **Ingredient 5 in a nutshell** | On the different levels of acceptance and support (e.g. communication and empowerment), several best practices are known to inform and motivate employees towards the usage of a BSC. For example trainings, key user programs and the right to say in a matter are profound methods to reach acceptance and support of the staff. Although this ingredient can only provide soft issues, it is often seen as the most important for the success of the whole approach. |

### 4.5.1 Definition

**Acceptance and support** is perhaps the best documented and most obvious ingredient in books and management trainings.

As an ingredient, this aspect will be defined in this context as considering all initiatives and approaches that help employees and managers to really accept the BSC as a concept (**acceptance**) and correspondingly use it successfully in everyday business (**support**). Even if the soft factors are predominant in this ingredient, the attempt will be made to derive components as specific as possible.

## 4.5.2 Background

Although supporting IT systems, reporting systems and other mechanisms are usually available for most projects and processes, the
relevant people need to support the concept of BSC and it is up to
them to keep it alive. Employees need to be motivated to work with
a BSC and need to be instructed to participate. Otherwise the project will fail in any case.

## 4.5.3 Components

Four components of acceptance and support constitute a kind of
maturity level as shown in figure 22: Achieving a higher level in this
model can be seen as related to reaching more acceptance and
support.

Figure 24: Maturity model for acceptance and support
[Source: own illustration]

### Commitment

Commitment describes the initial dedication of the management to
the BSC. This commitment is necessary at a very early stage within

the BSC introduction (Harber 1998) and essential for all subsequent steps (Value Competence Consulting 2002). Oftentimes this support is seen as particularly critical because a lack of managerial support will entail a lack of support at employee level (Richardson 2004; Value Competence Consulting 2002; Kaplan and Norton 2001; Hyperspace 2010; Blackall 2007).

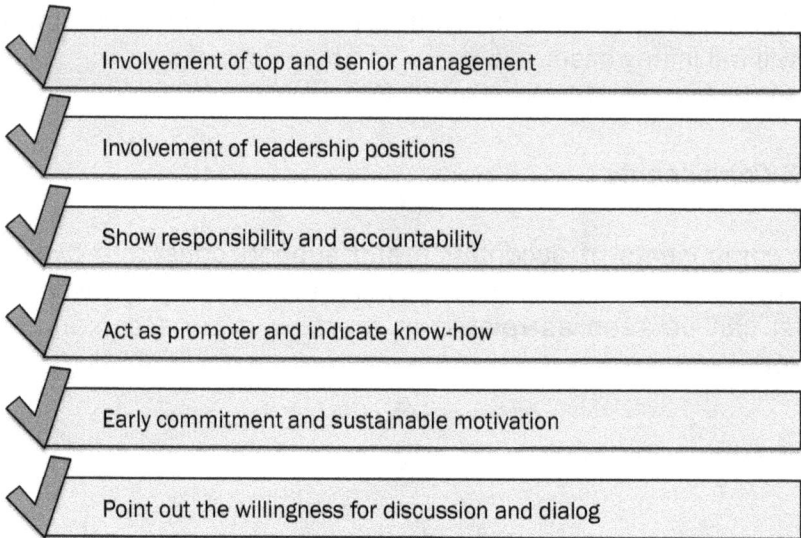

Figure 25: Characteristics of a successful commitment
[Source: own illustration]

Figure 25 summarizes the essential characteristics of a successful commitment: The top management must be involved in the project and process of the BSC and has to take the responsibility (Vohl 2004). The senior and middle management have to stand behind the BSC as a management concept and have to promote its objectives in a conceptual as well as in a practical way (Weber and Schäffer 2000). Thus, at the beginning all positions with leadership tasks must commit to the BSC. In a next step, a top-down series can be started to pass on motivation.

Managers need to become and stay promoters for the concepts (Hyperspace 2010; Weber and Schäffer 2000). A single supporter is not sufficient, but the entire management of the BSC needs to be committed (Value Competence Consulting 2002).

In addition to cross-functional commitment, methodological knowledge of the management as well as the ability to pass on know-how is another essential aspect (Weber and Schäffer 2000; Hyperspace 2010). Assertive messages need to be communicated to the staff in order to generate a positive attitude towards the BSC (Value Competence Consulting 2002). Involvement of employees will also prepare the organization for subsequent stages of the maturity model and can mobilize for change (Hendricks, Menor and Wiedmann 2004; Kaplan and Norton 2001). As early as possible, commitment should be closely related to the upcoming project (PricewaterhouseCoopers n.d.) and widely communicated (Morisawa and Kurosaki 2003; Harber 1998). To maintain long-term motivation, commitment must also be prevail in later phases (Hyperspace 2010).

### Communication

Communication is understood as the distribution of necessary information. Even if feedback options are available, this aspect aims at a more extensive spreading of BSC-related information that should be clear and understandable for everyone (Kaplan and Norton 1996; PricewaterhouseCoopers n.d.). A lack of communication can have a lasting negative impact on the further acceptance and promotion by employees (Mair 2002; Richardson 2004; Pandey 2005; Schermann and Volcic 2009).

The first communication of content, such as the commitment of managers, the general objectives of the BSC, its vision and mission as well as the strategy map should take place before the actual introduction (Bauer 2010). Although, after some time, communication will change in terms of content, it should be pursued continuously as a reminder that the management still takes the BSC seriously (Angel and Rampersad 2005). A common terminology can ensure that all parties have the same idea of the desired overall BSC goals (Niven 2002; Morisawa and Kurosaki 2003). Only if the company's vision and mission are clearly formulated and communicated (Hyperspace 2010), the overall project can be understood (see also next level of the maturity model).

Besides the goal of spreading knowledge, communication should also focus on the promotion of acceptance and the reduction of anxiety (Vohl 2004; Hyperspace 2010). Therefore it is necessary that the communication by the top management makes absolutely clear that the BSC is not an additional control tool and will not create **transparent staff** (Hyperspace 2010). In order to achieve an understanding by employees, the communication channels should be adjusted appropriately to the audience (Williams 2004). Overall, an open atmosphere and open information policy is needed (Schmeisser and Clausen 2009; Weber and Schäffer 2000). The responsibility for effective communication lies on all managers and leaders, but in particular on the top management (Bauer 2010).

### Understanding

Understanding describes that employees are motivated and committed, have received all necessary information (from communication) and now experience the BSC by interaction. Belief in the BSC is critical for project success and change in the company culture (Hendricks, Menor and Wiedmann 2004). The understanding of the BSC can provide the necessary acceptance for then using the BSC as a guideline for everyday work (Richardson 2004).

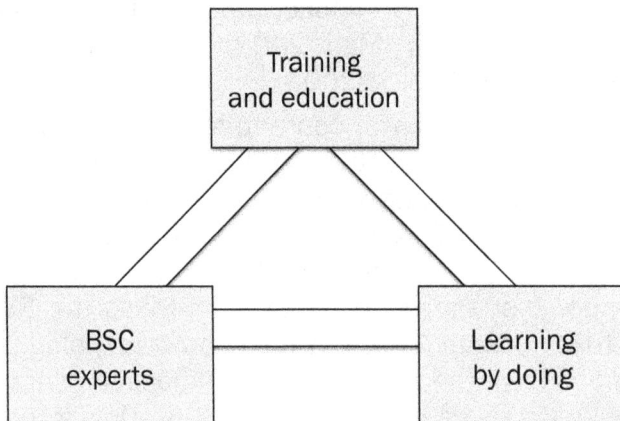

Figure 26: Methods for gaining understanding

[Source: own illustration]

Three basic methods are known to increase the understanding of the BSC (see also figure 24).

The first method is to provide **training and education** for the employees so that they can learn how to handle the BSC (Niven 2002). A lack of training or advice can result in immense resistance (Hyperspace 2010; Niven 2002). Within trainings, employees should learn all aspects which are relevant for their work (Williams 2004). Like this, their trust in the concept will increase successively (PricewaterhouseCoopers n.d.). Moreover, particular attention should also be paid to qualifications on strategy, the use of a common language and an appropriate visualization (Peters 2008; Crespo et al. 2009). Training is necessary for both line employees as well as managerial staff (Blackall 2007).

The second method is **learning by doing**: It can support employees to find their way in dealing with the BSC when they are allowed to make mistakes during the initial phase and when at first the incentive systems are not integrated yet (PricewaterhouseCoopers n.d.). Continuous self-study can help to handle key indicators, reporting and initiatives (Bauer 2010).

The third method is using **BSC experts**: Employees with a high level of knowledge and information about all aspects of the BSC should be available. Experts are important and should serve as promoters and supporters throughout the organization at any time. These experts will be needed in the operational departments as well as for the entire organization (Morisawa and Kurosaki 2003).

### Empowerment

In this context, empowerment describes that employees at various levels acquire autonomy to influence or even design parts of their BSC. The lack of empowerment can turn out to be particularly fatal in BSC projects (Mair 2002). In addition to the willingness to design, employees need to understand the BSC concept. The level of **empowerment** is generally seen as the highest level of **acceptance and support**.

An open atmosphere and a considerate and friendly attitude towards colleagues is the basis of empowerment (Weber and Schäffer 2000). Employees will only contribute in a pleasant and positive work environment, where leadership is based on a considerate and friendly attitude towards all colleagues (PricewaterhouseCoopers n.d.; Schermann and Volcic 2009). Distrust, suspiciousness, and carelessness characterize an undesirable mentality (Angel and Rampersad 2005).

Participation in the concept can be initiated in different ways. A professional team of moderators can be used to guide employees who have the abilities to participate in the concept (Hyperspace 2010). Another starting point is training. Workshops can lead to new insights and BSC results (Crespo et al. 2009). Moreover, workshops can also be used to re-check strategy and to collect contributions by individual employees (Bodmer and Völker 2000; Bauer 2010). Another possible form of participation is to negotiate target agreements based on the BSC (Bauer 2010). The process of reaching agreements together ensures that individual employees have the opportunity to contribute to the objectives and can, at least in part, actively shape them, which is one of the key success factors (Peters 2008). Equally, creative techniques, such as brainstorming, are good means to generate new ideas, strategies and measures. Another possibility to encourage active commitment to the BSC is to discuss openly in all BSC workshops (Niven 1998; Bauer 2010).

### 4.5.4 Advantages

At the various levels, numerous advantages of this ingredient are already named; therefore these statements should not be repeated.

The most important conclusion of this ingredient is that the participants of an organization must accept and support the BSC concept.

### 4.5.5 Limitations and Restrictions

The management needs to check in the planning phase as well as in the implementation of all actions on the different levels of the maturity model, if the introduction of the BSC and the associated benefits actually exceed the costs for this ingredient. If the expenditures on soft factors and human resources are too high, the BSC project must be waived.

This ingredient shows that the four described levels have to be taken into account in any case. Without acceptance and support of the employees, the BSC cannot be brought to life.

### 4.5.6 Introduction

For various reasons, a general and universal introduction plan of this ingredient cannot be given. Every company has to establish individual plans to implement this ingredient:

- The nature of the maturity level depends to a large extent on the type of staff. Whereas some lower-level employee's empowerment is not necessary at all or only in later stages of the BSC, the employees of the BSC core team need to be on the same level in the first stage of the project.
- Soft factors vary enormously from company to company. Whether training, learning by doing and open communication are applicable in a particular company, must be decided individually. Companies that have already introduced many of the components stated as necessary for a successful operation can certainly enter the process at a higher level.
- Corporate cultures are complex and often general implications are thus difficult to describe.

As a basic trend, it can be concluded that the question of commitment and communication is important at the early stages. They need to be initiated before the introduction of the BSC in any case (Value Competence Consulting 2002). Questions of understanding could be particularly relevant in the beginning of the launch, because afterwards employees will be actually working with the BSC. Empowerment probably plays a role in the later phases. For example, active participation can be helpful in the refinement phase, when the BSC begins to affect the environment of individual employees.

### 4.5.7 Example of Application

#### Corporate Level

Efforts to promote the BSC concept will only work if the concept is accepted and supported by the employees. For this reasons, ingredient 5 recommends that employee motivation is explicitly addressed by fostering commitment, communication, understanding and empowerment.

*Commitments*

As described above, commitment needs to be clearly communicated in the early stage of the BSC introduction and renewed continuously. In the case of ABC it was communicated at two levels:

- **Management board:** The management board of ABC committed to the BSC and its components as well as to the described ingredients. At the first introduction of the BSC, the importance and motivation was presented on the intranet under the heading of corporate information and communicated in the first BSC workshop. In the typical intranet style of articles by the management board, the importance of the concept was explained.
- **Process owners:** The heads of process teams presented their commitment to the BSC in the workshops, in the target agreement meetings as well as in the daily work.

Each commitment, either in writing, on the intranet or in the presentation, contained all described components, which were quite necessary for the meaningfulness of the statement.

*Communication*

Communication prescribes that employees (including their leaders) of ABC are informed about the BSC. In detail, the following recommendations were made:

- **Intranet:** The strategy management was presented in the intranet. In addition to contact details, documents (e. g. forms), slides (e. g. BSC user training), links (e. g. to the BSC SharePoint), statements (e. g. commitment from the management board) and other information (e. g. presentation of the BSC processes, glossary) were made available.
- **Senior management committee:** The BSC became a mandatory part of the presentation of the process activities at senior management committee meetings. This target-to-one comparison can on the one hand be used to describe the current challenges and activities of the process, and on the other hand this type of communication ensures that the meeting content follows the vision and corporate strategy of ABC.
- **Meetings in general:** The BSC of processes was used as information in staff meetings. In this way, the BSC became a self-evident part of the department's communication style (e. g. in an annual department workshop).

Of course, there were also many other possible communication activities (e. g. in in-house magazine, posters on black boards, etc.).

*Understanding*

To support understanding, as stated in ingredient 5, three different thematic aspects were addressed: BSC training, learning by doing possibilities and the provision of BSC experts. From the overall application of the ingredients, three levels of **training** resulted for ABC (detailed recommendations for content of these trainings can be found in appendix A.10):

- **BSC Introduction:** For new employees, each department or process group had the option of giving a brief presentation on important issues. In this context, strategy management gave a brief introduction on the BSC concept and understanding of ABC.

- **BSC User:** All employees who are affected by the BSC received trainings regarding the concept. In particular, training contents focused on how employees can contribute to the BSC of the process and how they can profit from their personal BSC.
- **BSC Expert:** This training was hosted by strategy management and tailored to train heads of departments, process owners, and employees in charge of the departments. After this intensive training, participants had all necessary skills to implement the cascading and the application of the BSC for their own process groups or in their own departments. Another important aim was to convince the participants about the benefits of the approach and to create enthusiasm for the strategy-driven framework. The hired experts played a key role in conveying the commitment and advantages to the departments and processes.

The strategy management team participated in further external training courses to stay open-minded for general new developments in the area of performance management and BSC.

Gaining experience was possible for all employees in a six-month test run period (**learning by doing**) at each implementation level. Employees learned about the functioning of the BSC without incurring negative consequences for their process or for themselves. Managers appropriately communicated the explicit goals of the test runs.

It is recommended to provide **BSC experts** to all employees of ABC, whereby the experts are available to respond to general, technical, methodicalm and personal questions about the BSC. In any case, strategy management was a potential partner for all employees and process teams. In addition, the process owners (or delegated staff) were able to offer support for technical and methodological issues in the processes since he or she attended the BSC expert training.

*Empowerment*

In the last step, employees were given an opportunity to influence the design and content of the BSC. This was achieved within the processes and departments by participation in the introduction or review and improvement workshops.

The responsible process owner or a delegated employee also organized a feedback session. This session provided the opportunity to collect and discuss opinions and wishes of employees and submit this feedback to the BSC workshops on corporate level.

Employees could, however, directly influence their personal BSC at the annual target agreement meeting.

## Process level

In the pilot project of the logistic process, all involved employees were highly motivated. They have adapted and critically reflected the concept.

*Commitment*

The process owner of the logistic process committed himself clearly to the concept of the BSC as well as to the ingredient in the kick-off. He handed over the responsibility to a team leader with managerial responsibility after the kick-off. He has nevertheless shown his commitment and interest in the developed results on a continuous basis.

*Communication*

Required and formal information such as the ingredients were provided in a presentation during the kick-off. In all meetings, only those terms which met the specialized instructions of the process were used, and newly introduced terms were described and explained.

*Understanding*

The BSC workshops were comprehensively used to analyze which strategic objectives are needed to fulfill the vision of logistics. Existing activities were systematically questioned, and the discussion discovered many internal optimization opportunities. The clear approach to develop all results in a strategy-oriented manner generated a lot of employee support. Particularly the process team could profit from the strategy map, because employees described the strategy of the entire process for the first time in a uniform formula. In the BSC, however, current problems of the process team were addressed and the requirements of the employees, who did not previously appear in the reports, were considered (soft measures). The employees had to understand that the BSC outlines what management is actually expecting from them. For this purpose, surely also the created personal BSCs can provide a significant contribution. These personal BSCs were distributed to the staff (see example in appendix A.8).

In order to adequately train employees on the new management concept, it is recommended that the process team participate in the BSC user training sessions (described on corporate level). The acting process owner can act as a BSC expert and can promote the BSC within the entire process. These experienced participants from the pilot run in the logistic organization moreover participated in the development of the BSC expert trainings on corporate level, in order to make these training courses user-friendly.

*Empowerment*

The recommendations given at the corporate level were also implemented for the logistic process team accordingly.

## 4.6    Ingredient 6: Continuous Process

| For the quick reader | |
| --- | --- |
| **Fundamental spice** | "Make strategy a continual process." Kaplan and Norton 2001 |
| **Ingredient 6 in a nutshell** | After the BSC is introduced, cascaded and integrated into an organization, a continuous process needs to be started in which the BSC is updated, corrected and improved. The described review and improvement activities can help to establish the BSC as a lasting and effective instrument for strategic management. |

### 4.6.1 Definition

The term **process** already indicates that this ingredient describes the BSC as a running (**continuous**) approach, unlike the introduction project (see ingredient 1). Typical input to this process is internal and external knowledge, experiences and market changes to be considered in the BSC. Output of the ingredient are implications to adjust and improve the BSC, and thus guidelines to improve the BSC as a management concept.

### 4.6.2 Background

The demand for constant development and improvement is already formulated in the basic recipe: Key claim of the BSC is that it develops actionable indicators based on a strategy (Kaplan and Norton 1996). Since this strategy can change at any time, the BSC has to adapt to these changes by analyzing them conceptually as well as practically (Kaplan and Norton 2001; Hyperspace 2010).

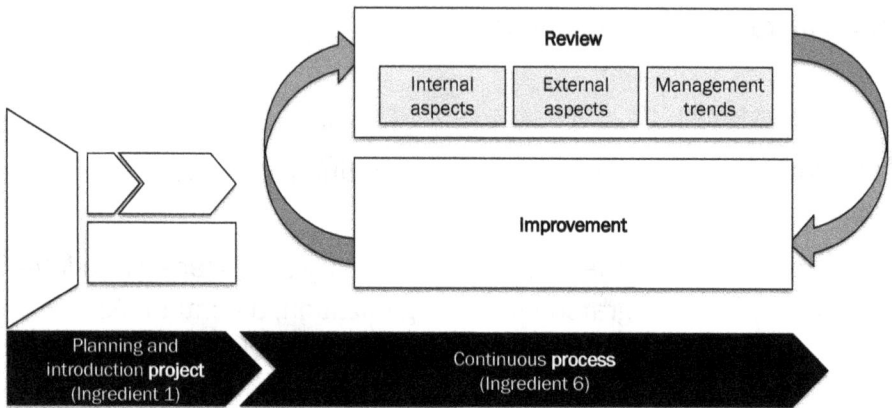

Figure 27: Continuous process of the BSC after the introduction project
[Source: own illustration]

All aspects of this ingredient have in common that they see an ongoing process after the first introductory and planning project. This process is supposed to include activities of checking, changing, adaptation, updating and redesign (Hendricks, Menor and Wiedmann 2004; Bauer 2010; Othman et al. 2006; Williams 2004; Hyperspace 2010, Morisawa and Kurosaki 2003). The transition from a **project** to a **continuous process** is depicted in figure 27: After the planning and introduction project, the knowledge gained from a review can be used to improve the management of the BSC. This will lead to a continuous process of enhancement.

### 4.6.3 Components

It should be noted that all descriptions of the aspects and approaches put forward are very generic, because the conceptual and practical tasks set by this ingredient differ, of course, according to the BSC which is actually implemented. Essentially, all aspects are classified into two major fields, i. e. **review** and **improvement**. Both components need to be run iteratively to secure the long-term use of the BSC.

### Review Process

A review can consider both internal and external aspects as well as general management trends.

- **Internally,** the perception of the assumptions on which the BSC is based must be reviewed regularly (Ghosh and Mukherjee 2006; Hyperspace 2010). Since the BSC is also a permanent link to the company's strategy process and as strategy can change, the BSC needs to be updated whenever the strategy framework changes (Ghosh and Mukherjee 2006; Niven 2002). If internal conditions, which influence assumptions and strategy, change, these conditions as well as resulting aspects have to be improved (Harber 1998). In business practice typically new figures, available data or new descriptions are changing and require the alignment of the BSC (Harber 1998; Williams 2004).
- **External** aspects of review describe the continuous check if the BSC is consistent with the environment of the company. Changes in environmental conditions can have an impact on the content and structure of the BSC (Othman et al. 2006). The reason for this review necessity is that a BSC is based on specific cause-effect relationships (Othman et al. 2006) and thus also on specific hypotheses about the environment (Morisawa and Kurosaki 2003). This implies that necessary changes and improvements of the BSC can also be based on external factors (Peters 2008).
- **Trends** must also be considered during the review process. Depending on focus, importance and relevance of new management trends, several different factors are necessary to improve the BSC.

### Improvement Process

Improvement can be regarded on two levels in a continuous process: If areas for changes and new aspects are recorded in the review, corresponding improvements need to be made. New or updated measures or an adapted structure of the BSC are among the results of the BSC approach. In addition, changes for additional improvements are also planned. The overall suggestion is to gradually extend the integration with other existing business concepts (see also ingredient 2). It does not make sense at the beginning to combine incentives with a BSC, but this integration has to be increased only gradually (PricewaterhouseCoopers). In the continuous process, the BSC needs to stabilize first by developing links with information processes, business processes, and performance evaluation (Bodmer and Völker 2000). In addition, the insights gained from the previous BSC operation should be recorded as part of a learning process (Ringe 2006).

### 4.6.4 Advantages

The continuous process offers numerous advantages. The following aspects are essential:

- If a BSC is not adequately supervised and updated, employees will boycott the concept quickly. The continuous process offers a way out and can help that employees continue all initiatives (Hyperspace 2010).
- The view that the BSC is an ongoing process leads learning effects (Ringe 2006; Schmeisser and Clausen 2009).
- When the connection with other business concepts is extended, this trend is associated with numerous integration benefits (Hendricks, Menor and Wiedmann 2004). These aspects can be found in detail in the documentation of ingredient 2.
- In a review, indicators and initiatives are reflected in a critical way. Necessary aspects for the consideration of new facets can be implemented (Niven 1998).
- The continuous reviewing of a BSC makes employees recognizing and understanding its value and importance. In this way, the BSC can effectively become part of the daily work (Richardson 2004).

### Limitations and Restrictions

Restrictions for the usage of the continuous process are not available. The establishment of a continuous process therefore appears to be recommendable in any case of an ongoing BSC execution.

Limits result primarily from variation of the intensity of the degree of implementation of the continuous process. Figure 28 depicts exemplary arguments in favor and against an intensive process of review and improvement.

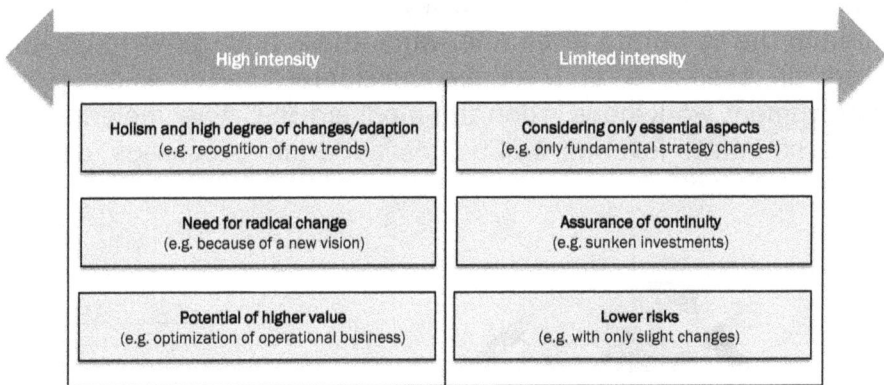

| High intensity | Limited intensity |
|---|---|
| Holism and high degree of changes/adaption (e.g. recognition of new trends) | Considering only essential aspects (e.g. only fundamental strategy changes) |
| Need for radical change (e.g. because of a new vision) | Assurance of continuity (e.g. sunken investments) |
| Potential of higher value (e.g. optimization of operational business) | Lower risks (e.g. with only slight changes) |

Figure 28: Continuum of intensity of the continuous process
[Source: own illustration]

## 4.6.5 Introduction

The continuous process should begin immediately after the implementation project is completed. It is important to set fixed intervals for the continuous process, permitting review and improvement (for example, once at the end of the year to optimize and align the strategy-driven activities for the following business year).

It is also important to note that the described process can be performed ad hoc, whenever fundamental vision and strategy adjustments are necessary, when changes in the corporate organization appear, or when other major key parameters change.

## 4.6.6 Example of Application

### Corporate Level

Ingredient 6 notes that the BSC project has to become an ongoing and continuous process. The BSC is optimized continuously regarding its contents (e. g. objectives and measures) and methodology (e. g. techniques for cascading).

Figure 29 is based on the process described in the ingredient and enriches it with specific aspects of ABC: Different sources of information were analyzed in a review workshop after the BSC was executed at the corporate level. Afterwards these findings were consolidated in scenarios and will be considered in the subsequent improvement workshops. Then the modified BSC was implemented at the corporate level as well as cascaded into processes, departments and teams.

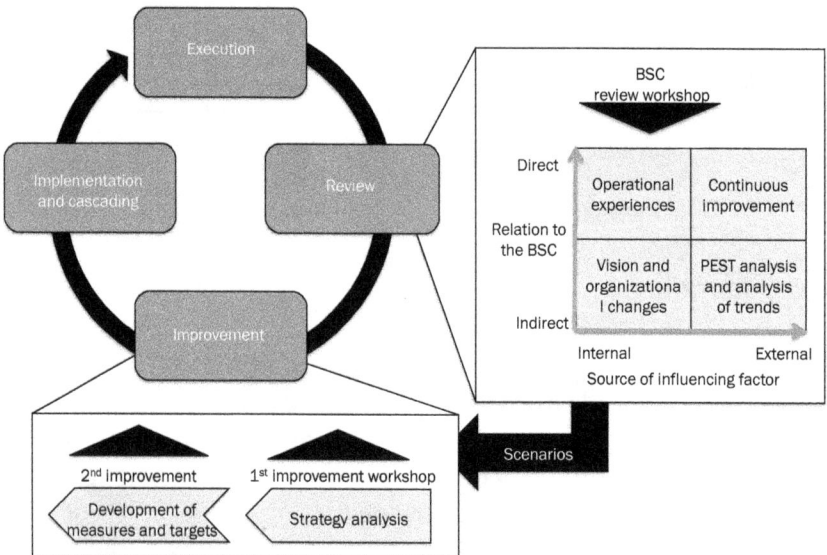

Figure 29: Continuous process of the BSC for ABC
[Source: own illustration]

In the following, specific lessons learned and applications for the review and improvement of the continuous process are made with respect to ABC.

*Review*

Before the BSC improvement workshops have been performed, ABC conducted a review workshop. This workshop aimed to achieve two goals: First, the previous BSC executions as well as other internal and external information were reflected in a critical manner. Second, this workshop provided information required for the effective continuous improvement of the BSC.

Ingredient 6 describes that both internal as well as external aspects should be taken into account during the review. Internal aspects result from the company itself, while external aspects originate from the relevant external environment. In the case of ABC, direct and indirect information sources were also added (see portfolio in figure 29): Direct information is highly connected with the BSC (e. g. experiences with the cascading) while indirect information is not primarily connected with the BSC (e. g. general political changes that influence the strategic objectives). The following aspects were dealt with in the review workshop (a recommended agenda for the workshop can be found in appendix A.9):

- **Operational experiences**: The experience of the BSC operation within ABC in the last year were discussed and analyzed. By doing so, internal learning effects could be achieved and the BSC was gradually improved.
- **Continuous improvement**: Strategy management had the task of providing ongoing education in the area of performance management and BSC (e. g. training courses, seminars, research). The developed proposals for improvement were discussed in the workshop.
- **Vision and organizational changes**: The management board as delegated staff introduced relevant changes to the company's vision and the organizational design of ABC. This information was needed for an appropriate change of the strategic objectives.

- **PEST analysis and analysis of trends**: Since decisions of ABC are largely influenced by external factors, it was reasonable to do a comprehensive PEST analysis in small groups (PEST for political, economic, social, technological aspects). This framework and approach[11] was particularly appropriate for the application, because the PEST analysis is widely known as a very efficient method for identifying external influences in a company's environment, identifying the driving forces and estimating factors that influence the strategy (Pfaff 2004). In addition, strategy management presented identified relevant management trends (e.g. lean management, new CSR approaches), which were then evaluated in a discussion.

*Improvement*

The already outlined BSC introduction workshops can also be used for the continuous improvement of the BSC. Only the following changes were made in order to implement an effective improvement workshop:

- **Input**: In addition to the vision, the adopted findings of the review workshops (especially the developed scenarios for the company future) were input for the improvement workshops as well. Strategy management addressed the main findings of the previous meetings in the first workshop to set the stage. Other key inputs were the indicators, target results, strategic objectives and existing documentation of the previous BSC execution.
- **Strategy interviews**: This type of pre-survey of strategic goals could be waived, because the strategy management could forecast that the change and adaptation of existing objectives can be achieved within the time frame of the first workshop.
- **Timing**: The timing of the workshops needed to be changed according to partially modified inputs, processes and results.

---

11    Details on and implementation guidelines for the PEST framework can be found in Fahey and Narayanan (1986).

For example, the elaboration of the strategic objectives was accelerated by the fact that objectives already existed.

- **Workshop type**: Since the methodological skills and knowledge of participants will grow within the continuous process year by year, strategy management can allow for more discussions and group work by the participants in the workshops.

The third BSC workshop, in which the implementation (e. g. cascading) is explained, can be waived in the continuous process because these contents should be documented after the first process cycle as binding technical instructions (e. g. available on the intranet).

### Process Level

The continuous process suggested in the application of ingredient 6 should be used on the level of business processes. The strategy management team presented and discussed the concept of the continuous process as well as the developed agendas of the workshops in detail with the process owner as well as with managerial staff in the process. All participants of the workshops agreed to use these BSC workshops in the future. The described review and improvement workshops took place at the end of the fiscal year, the BSC was introduced, for the first time.

# 5 Summary and Conclusion

> *I think it is important and right to self-implement
> strategies, and I can only recommend any company,
> to not allow a break between the conceptual design
> and the implementation.*

GRUBE 2005[12]

Unlike many other management concepts, the BSC constitutes a possible bridge for the gap between strategic or visionary plans on the one side and the actual operational implementation on the other side. After the presentation of vision and strategy in its strategy map, the BSC is able to translate this long-term view into operational and measureable actions. The BSC thus takes effect at the exact spot which Grube called for in 2005: The BSC avoids a break.

As described in the basic recipe, the original form of the BSC, however, often reaches its limits and implies various risks: Actually, in about two thirds of all businesses and organizations, the BSC is not fully implemented as a performance management framework and its potential to design the described bridge is therefore lost. Instead, it often degenerates into a short-term reporting instrument and thus its characteristics valuable for a balanced system, straightforward learning, strategy-oriented coordination, leadership of employees, and alignment of the entire enterprise to reach the vision, cannot be implemented. The BSC loses its power to prevent the rupture between vision and strategy and operational activities.

---

[12] Rüdiger Grube was at the time of the citation senior vice president at DaimlerChrysler, today he is CEO of the Deutsche Bahn AG. The statement is taken from an interview with FAZ (2005).

This cookbook was able to document delicious ingredients for successful BSCs. All generic guidelines have been equipped with specific recommendations for business practice, on what constitutes a successful and modern BSC.

A successful BSC requires a phase of systematic planning and introduction (ingredient 1), a phase of comprehensive integration (ingredient 2) as well as a phase of cascading into the existing organization (ingredient 3) and a good design of measures (ingredient 4). Moreover, it is particularly important to build up trust, acceptance and support (ingredient 5) and to continually review and improve the BSC (ingredient 6).

Also in the case of application to ABC these ingredient could show, how successful the concept of the BSC as well as how successful and important the contribution of the developed ingredients was: A comprehensive management concept at corporate level as well as on the level of business processes was designed and implemented as well as integrated holistically into the company. This constitutes a tailored approach to efficient performance management. The novel concept has the potential to support companies, which are currently facing new and greater strategic challenges in the market.

A BSC which is introduced, operated and maintained according to these state-of-the-art principles has the potential to reduce further breaks by fitting the performance management perfectly into the organization and also by building bridges to a more modern management. The ingredients can thus help to pave the way to render one of the most successful business and management concepts of our days fit for the future.

# Appendix

## A    Templates

To complement the detailed explanations in the ingredients, the reader will find the most important templates that have been used in the case study of ABC in this chapter.

All templates can also be downloaded at www.process-transparency.com using the password *cooking* and can be used for your own projects.

## A.1  Kick-off Outline

| BSC Kick-off Meeting | |
|---|---|
| **Participants** | <ul><li>Management board</li><li>Members of the senior management committee</li><li>Employees of strategy management</li><li>Responsible employees of pilot projects</li><li>Heads of business groups</li><li>Heads of business units</li></ul> |
| **Proceeding**<br>(R = Responsible) | <ul><li>Welcome and general motivation of staff<br>*(R: strategy management)*</li><li>Commitment of management board<br>*(R: top management and strategy management)*</li><li>Presentation of participating groups and individuals<br>*(R: all participants)*</li><li>Presentation of ABC's vision at corporate level<br>*(R: top management or strategy management)*</li><li>Presentation of preliminary planning for the implementation project and information for the following strategy interviews<br>*(R: strategy management)*</li><li>Recap of the ABC's rules for cooperation in meetings and workshops<br>(R: *strategy management*)</li><li>Closing: Motivation of all participants based on two testimonials from experts about BSC<br>*(R: two internal employees act as experts )*</li></ul> |
| **Outcomes** | <ul><li>Objectives, content, deadlines and responsibilities for the BSC planning and rollout are communicated</li><li>Open issues or questions were resolved or recorded</li><li>Rules for efficient working together were accepted</li></ul> |
| **Time planning** | Two hours |

## A.2   Strategy Interview Outline

| BSC Strategy Interview (Strategy Analysis) | |
|---|---|
| **Participants** | ▪ Interviewer: Employee of strategy management<br>▪ Interviewee:<br>   o   Member of senior management committee or<br>   o   Head of business group or<br>   o   Head of business unit |
| **Proceeding**<br>(R = Responsible) | ▪ Introduction (10 minutes)<br>   o   Welcome<br>   o   Presentation and description of the interview aims<br>▪ Vision explanation (10 minutes)<br>   o   Recapitulation of the communicated vision of ABC<br>▪ Strategic objectives within perspectives (60 minutes)<br><br><br><br>   o   Naming of strategic goals within all BSC perspectives by the interviewee<br>   o   Short description of the contents of each objective by the interviewee<br>   o   Prioritization of the goals formulated by the interviewee<br>▪ Closing (10 minutes)<br>   o   Question regarding potential further interviewees and contacts<br>   o   Question regarding expectations from the BSC project<br>   o   Thanks for the interview |
| **Outcomes** | ▪ Documented strategic goals with a short description<br>▪ List of possible further contacts<br>▪ Documentation of individual expectations from the BSC project |
| **Time planning** | One and a half hours (each interview) |

## A.3    1st BSC Workshop Outline

| 1st BSC Workshop (Strategy Analysis) | |
|---|---|
| **Participants** | • Members of senior management committee<br>• Employees of strategy management<br>• Process owners/heads of departments or delegated employees |
| **Proceeding**<br>(R = responsible) | • Presentation of experience of the BSC pilot projects to set the stage and increase motivation<br>*(R: responsible employees from the processes)*<br>• Training of BSC fundamentals (e. g. BSC approach, success and further development principles, etc.)<br>*(R: strategy management)*<br>• Presentation of the results from the strategy interviews<br>*(R: strategy management)*<br>• Discussion of the content and importance of each objective<br>*(R: all participants, moderated discussion)*<br>• Agreement on and selection of the most important goals (maximum 20)<br>*(R: all participants, moderated discussion)*<br>• Classification of the goals in the perspectives (e. g. on several flip charts)<br>*(R: all participants, moderated discussion)*<br>• Completion with causal relationships<br>*(R: all participants, moderated discussion)*<br>• Closing: Thanks for participation and presentation of next steps<br>*(R: strategy management)* |
| **Type** | Presentation, followed by moderated discussion |
| **Outcomes** | • Agreed strategic objectives and common understanding of corporate strategy<br>• Strategy map at the corporate level<br>• First draft of a BSC |
| **Time planning** | One day |

## A.4　2nd BSC Workshop Outline

| 2nd BSC Workshop (Development of Measures and Targets) | |
|---|---|
| Participants | ■ Members of senior management committee<br>■ Employees of strategy management<br>■ Process owners/heads of departments or delegated employees |
| Proceeding<br>(R = responsible) | **First day**<br>■ Brief description of past results and status of the BSC approach<br>   *(R: strategy management)*<br>■ Presentation on the next steps<br>   *(R: strategy management and internal aspects)*<br>    o Instructions and methods for developing indicators and activities<br>    o Theories and practical advice for good measures (ingredient 4)<br>    o Presentation of forms (e. g. activity map) for documenting results (appendix I)<br>    o Presentation of the SharePoint system<br>■ Division of the whole group into cross-functional teams<br>   *(R: all participants in sub-groups)*<br>    o Each team works on a set of strategic objectives (e. g. within one perspective)<br>    o For each strategic objective, risks are documented<br>    o Each team appoints a leader who is responsible for the approach<br>    o The team coordinates its work on its own<br>■ During the preparation process, strategy management is available for questions concerning contents, process and methodology<br>   *(R: strategy management)*<br>■ Forms and results are displayed on the ABC SharePoint and documents are made available to all participants<br>   *(R: strategy management, groups)*<br>**Second day**<br>■ Wrap-up: Presentation of tips and hints for the documentation of measures and initiatives, clarification of frequently asked questions from day one<br>   *(R: strategy management and internal experts)*<br>■ The team continues working on measures and initiatives for the strategic objectives and documents results in the "strategic objective form" (appendix I)<br>   *(R: all participants in sub groups)*<br>■ The team leader of each group presents the group's results to all participants<br>   *(R: team leader)*<br>■ Discussion of all results and comparison with measurement aspects (balanced and compulsory)<br>   *(R: all participants, moderated discussion)* |

| | |
|---|---|
| | ▪ Completeness and consistency check as well as creation of the activity map<br>    *(R: all participants, moderated discussion)*<br>▪ Closing: Thanks for contribution<br>    *(R: strategy management)* |
| **Type** | Presentation, followed by team work and discussion |
| **Outcomes** | ▪ Completed and adopted activity map<br>▪ Completed strategic objective documentation forms<br>▪ Open issues list |
| **Time planning** | Two days |

## A.5 Strategic Objective Documentation Form

| BSC Strategic Objective | | | |
|---|---|---|---|
| Name of objective | | | |
| Identification number | | | |
| BSC reference | Process(es)/department(s) (according to initiative map) | | |
| | Perspective | | |
| Description | | | |
| Responsible person | | | |
| **Operationalization 1 (required)** | | | |
| Measure | Name | | . |
| | Nominator | | |
| | Denominator | | |
| | Frequency | | |
| | Description of measure and interpretation | | |
| | Data source | Nominator | |
| | | Denominator | |
| Targets | Current state | | |
| | Plan year 1 | | |
| | Plan year 2 | | |
| | Plan year 3 | | |
| Initiatives | Planned initiative | | Responsibility (employee or team) |
| | | | |
| | | | |
| | | | |
| **Operationalization 2 (optional)** | | | |
| (...) | (...) | | (...) |

## A.6 Example of a Measurement Card Form

| BSC Measurement Card | | |
|---|---|---|
| Name of measure | Turnover rate | |
| Identification number | 19-0023-01 | |
| BSC Reference | **Process** | Logistics |
| | **Perspective** | Partner (own employees) |
| | **Strategic objective** | Increase motivation |
| Interpretation | Employee satisfaction is measured as the number of employees who leave the process team at their own initiative in relation to the average number of employees. If this ratio decreases, a higher level of employee satisfaction was achieved, and vice versa. | |
| Definition of measure | **Numerator** | **Denominator** |
| | Number of departures | Average number of employees |
| Frequency of identification | Annually | |
| Source and verification | **Numerator** | **Denominator** |
| | Meeting protocol | Annual HR analysis |
| Responsible for data input | D. F., logistic process team lead | |
| Values and targets | | |

| | | Year 1 | Year 2 | Year 3 | Year 4 |
|---|---|---|---|---|---|
| **Period** | | Year 1 | Year 2 | Year 3 | Year 4 |
| Target | | 15% | 10% | 5% | 5% |
| As is | | 20% | | | |

| State of initiatives | **Name** | **Degree of completion** |
|---|---|---|
| | Organization of regular JFs | 100% |
| | Implement feedback sessions for team leads | 60% |
| | Increase number of persons in the development center | 0% |
| New initiatives | (...) | (...) |
| Last BSC review | October | |

## A.7  Target Agreement Form

| BSC Target Agreement for Employees | | |
|---|---|---|
| Employee Information | Name of employee | |
| | Employee ID | |
| | Name of executive | |
| Validity | Fiscal year | |
| Instructions | In this form, the targets agreement for the coming fiscal year are arranged with the employee. The BSC of the department/process, as derived from the parent corporate BSC, should form the basis for this agreement. | |
| | | |
| | When designing the goals, you should pay attention to the following: | |
| | 1. Try to balance the BSC perspectives. | |
| | 2. Consider the path of goal attainment as well as risks. | |
| | 3. If none of the measures in the process/department BSC can be applied, try to make the initiatives measurable (in this case pay attention to the requirements of good measures). | |
| | 4. The employee must be able to directly influence all measures. | |
| | If you have any questions, do not hesitate to contact strategy management. | |
| Commitment goal 1 | | |
| Name | | |
| Description and measure | | |
| BSC reference | Strategic objective ID | |
| | Perspective | |

| Target | Date | |
|---|---|---|
| | Minimum | |
| | Target | |
| | Maximum | |
| | Weighting | |
| **Commitment goal 2** | | |
| **Name** | | |
| **Description and measure** | | |
| **BSC reference** | Strategic objective ID | |
| | Perspective | |
| **Target** | Date | |
| | Minimum | |
| | Target | |
| | Maximum | |
| | Weighting | |
| **Commitment goal 3** | | |
| **Name** | | |
| **Description and measure** | | |
| **BSC reference** | Strategic objective ID | |
| | Perspective | |
| **Target** | Date | |
| | Minimum | |
| | Target | |
| | Maximum | |
| | Weighting | |
| **Commitment goal 4** | | |
| **Name** | | |
| **Description and measure** | | |
| **BSC reference** | Strategic objective ID | |
| | Perspective | |
| **Target** | Date | |
| | Minimum | |
| | Target | |
| | Maximum | |
| | Weighting | |

## A.8 Personal BSC Form

| Personal BSC of #Employee Name# (#ID#) |
|---|

### Vision

| Company vision | |
|---|---|
| Vision of process | |

### Financial

| Objective | Target | Initiative |
|---|---|---|
| | | |
| | | |
| | | |
| | | |

### Sustainability

| Objective | Target | Initiative |
|---|---|---|
| | | |
| | | |
| | | |
| | | |

### Partner

| Objective | Target | Initiative |
|---|---|---|
| | | |
| | | |
| | | |
| | | |

### Business processes and projects

| Objective | Target | Initiative |
|---|---|---|
| | | |
| | | |
| | | |
| | | |

### Learning and growth

| Objective | Target | Initiative |
|---|---|---|
| | | |
| | | |
| | | |
| | | |

## A.9    BSC Review Workshop

| BSC Review Workshop | |
|---|---|
| **Participants** | ▪ Employees of strategy management<br>▪ Process owners/heads of departments or delegated employees |
| **Proceeding**<br>(R = responsible) | ▪ Brief description of the goals of the workshop<br>    *(R: strategy management)*<br>▪ Presentation of organizational changes or changes to the company's vision<br>    *(R: management board or delegated employee)*<br>▪ All participants discuss the implications of these internal changes (vision and organizational changes)<br>    *(R: all participants, moderated discussion)*<br>▪ Based on the execution of the BSC, feedback from the participants is discussed and recommendations for improvements are documented (operational experiences)<br>    *(R: all participants, moderated discussion)*<br>▪ Strategy management provides recommendations for specific optimizations (continuous improvement).<br>    *(R: strategy management)*<br>▪ Discussion of the recommendations<br>    *(R: all participants, moderated discussion)*<br>▪ Presentation of current management trends<br>    *(R: strategy management)*<br>▪ Discussion of the importance of trends (in the case of expected disagreement within the group, a Delphi method can be applied), followed by a discussion on ways to integrate these trends to the BSC<br>    *(R: all participants, moderated discussion)*<br>▪ Presentation on the functioning of a PEST analysis in general<br>    *(R: strategy management)*<br>▪ Dividing the participants in four groups according their skills and background for PEST analysis<br>    *(R: strategy management)*<br>    ○ Each team works on relevant contents for one of the four thematic fields<br>    ○ The team works under a team leader (for groups which work in methodologically demanding fields, the team leader can be from strategy management)<br>    ○ The team documents the results in an appropriate form (e. g. slides, flip charts) for the presentation to the entire group<br>    ○ During the preparation process, strategy management is available for questions concerning contents, process and methodology |

| | |
|---|---|
| | ▪ Each team leader will present the results of his or her small group in the entire group<br>    *(R: team leader)*<br>▪ All participants discuss the results of the small groups and agree on facts to be considered<br>    *(R: all participants, moderated discussion)*<br>▪ All participants design possible scenarios for the future and estimate probabilities<br>    *(R: all participants, moderated discussion)*<br>▪ Presentation of next steps and closing<br>    *(R: strategy management)* |
| **Type** | Presentation, team work and discussion, presentation and discussion |
| **Outcomes** | ▪ Documented information that must be considered in the BSC and improvement workshops<br>▪ Scenario list<br>▪ Open issues list |
| **Time planning** | One day |

## A.10 BSC Training Concept

### BSC Trainings

#### BSC Introduction

| | |
|---|---|
| **Target group** | ▪ New employees |
| **Presenter** | ▪ Strategy management |
| **Agenda** | ▪ Introduction<br>   *(e. g. BSC fundamentals, vision, corporate strategy)*<br>▪ Relevance of the BSC to new employees<br>   *(e. g. target agreement form and incentive system)*<br>▪ Strategy management<br>   *(e. g. responsibilities, contact data)* |
| **Time planning** | 15 minutes |

#### BSC User

| | |
|---|---|
| **Target group** | ▪ All employees |
| **Presenter** | ▪ BSC experts<br>▪ Strategy management |
| **Agenda** | ▪ BSC fundamentals<br>   *(e. g. commitment of the management board, commitment of the department head and process owner, functioning and importance of the BSC, motivation/opportunities and targets, prevention of fears)*<br>▪ BSC at the process level<br>   *(e. g. workshops in the process teams/departments, methodology)*<br>▪ BSC on a personal level<br>   *(e. g. personal BSC form, target agreement and incentive system)* |
| **Time planning** | 2 hours |

#### BSC Expert

| | |
|---|---|
| **Target group** | ▪ BSC workshop participants (e. g. heads of departments/process owners or delegated employees)<br>▪ Responsible team leader for employees |
| **Presenter** | ▪ Strategy management<br>▪ Different experts for management frameworks<br>   *(e. g. corporate communication for strategy documentation, corporate IT for explanations on Microsoft SharePoint)* |
| **Agenda** | ▪ ABC's understanding of the BSC<br>   *(e. g. corporate strategy map, long-term definition of strategic objectives, BSC rules, commitment of the management board, workshop structure of ABC)* |

| | |
|---|---|
| | • Important management frameworks<br><br>*(e. g. meeting rules, tools for the motivation of employees, information security)*<br>• The BSC approach<br><br>*(e. g. examples for the BSC approach for ABC from vision to initiatives)*<br>• Success and further development principles<br><br>*(e. g. criteria for good measures)*<br>• Application and implementation within ABC<br><br>*(e. g. methods for cascading, contents of the BSC workshops, document handling in SharePoint)*<br>• ABC BSC experts<br><br>*(e. g. explanation of role, training for BSC user training, practical tips)*<br>• Further information<br><br>*(e. g. intranet information, contact details)* |
| **Time planning** | One day |

## A.11  BSC Risk Management Forms

### BSC Structural Risks

| BSC Reference | Process | |
| --- | --- | --- |
| | Perspective | |

| Endogenous risks | | | |
| --- | --- | --- | --- |
| Description | Preventative actions | Response actions | Impact on target achievement |
| | | | |
| | | | |
| | | | |

| Exogenous risks | | | |
| --- | --- | --- | --- |
| Description | Preventative actions | Response actions | Impact on target achievement |
| | | | |
| | | | |
| | | | |

### BSC Action-based Risks

| Name of initiative | | |
| --- | --- | --- |
| BSC Reference | Process | |
| | Perspective | |

| Strategic risks | | | |
| --- | --- | --- | --- |
| Description | Preventative actions | Response actions | Impact on target achievement |
| | | | |
| | | | |
| | | | |

| Operational risks | | | |
| --- | --- | --- | --- |
| Description | Preventative actions | Response actions | Impact on target achievement |
| | | | |
| | | | |
| | | | |

## A.12 Strategy Map of the Logistic Process

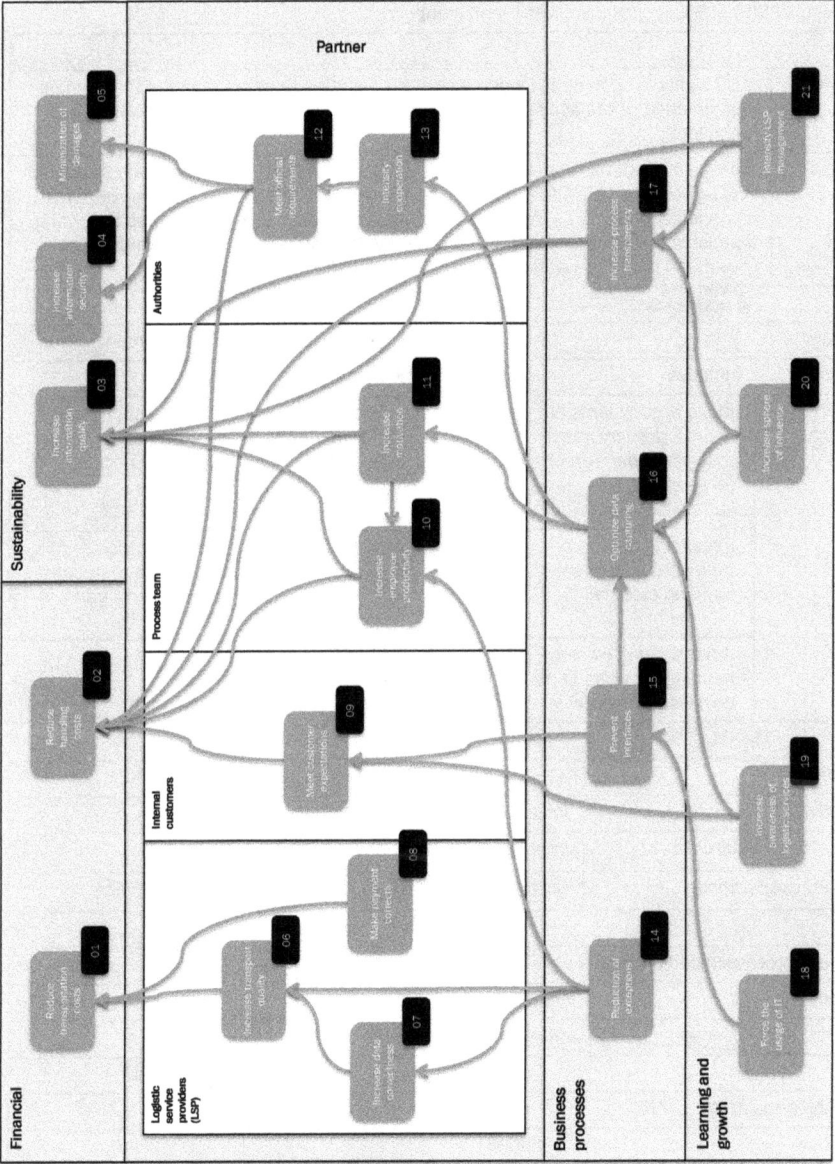

## A.13 Example of a Personal BSC

Personal BSC of B.L. (Logistic process team member)

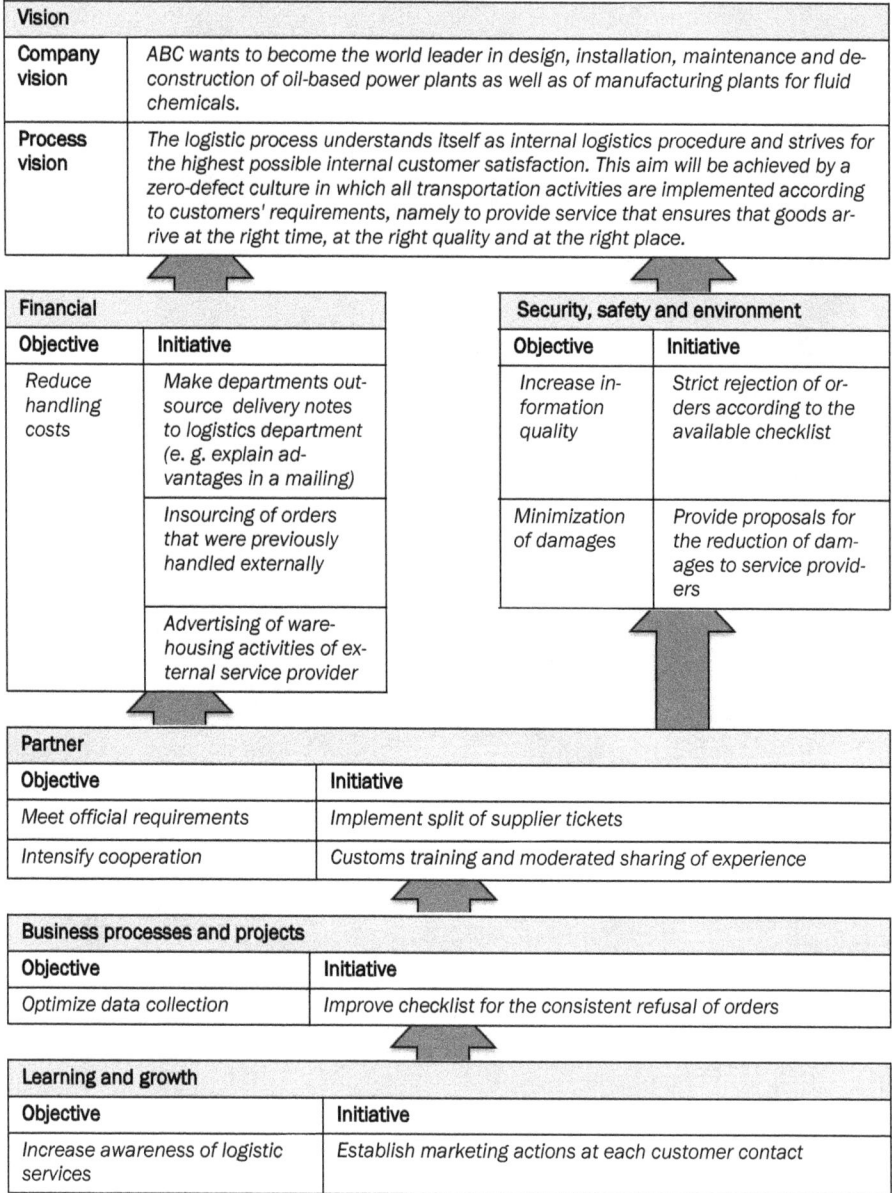

| Vision | |
|---|---|
| **Company vision** | *ABC wants to become the world leader in design, installation, maintenance and de-construction of oil-based power plants as well as of manufacturing plants for fluid chemicals.* |
| **Process vision** | *The logistic process understands itself as internal logistics procedure and strives for the highest possible internal customer satisfaction. This aim will be achieved by a zero-defect culture in which all transportation activities are implemented according to customers' requirements, namely to provide service that ensures that goods arrive at the right time, at the right quality and at the right place.* |

| Financial | |
|---|---|
| **Objective** | **Initiative** |
| *Reduce handling costs* | *Make departments out-source delivery notes to logistics department (e. g. explain advantages in a mailing)* |
| | *Insourcing of orders that were previously handled externally* |
| | *Advertising of warehousing activities of external service provider* |

| Security, safety and environment | |
|---|---|
| **Objective** | **Initiative** |
| *Increase information quality* | *Strict rejection of orders according to the available checklist* |
| *Minimization of damages* | *Provide proposals for the reduction of damages to service providers* |

| Partner | |
|---|---|
| **Objective** | **Initiative** |
| *Meet official requirements* | *Implement split of supplier tickets* |
| *Intensify cooperation* | *Customs training and moderated sharing of experience* |

| Business processes and projects | |
|---|---|
| **Objective** | **Initiative** |
| *Optimize data collection* | *Improve checklist for the consistent refusal of orders* |

| Learning and growth | |
|---|---|
| **Objective** | **Initiative** |
| *Increase awareness of logistic services* | *Establish marketing actions at each customer contact* |

## A.14 BSC of the Logistic Process

| Process BSC | | | |
|---|---|---|---|
| **BSC reference** | | | |
| Responsible person | D. F., Team lead | | |
| Identification number | BSC LP 01 | | |
| Date | Year 1 | | |
| **Strategic objective** | **Measure** | | **Initiatives** |
| **Financial perspective** | | | |
| 01 Reduce transport costs | Revenue per ton and kilometer: $$\frac{Total\ sales\ of\ LSPs}{Tons\ multiplied\ with\ the\ number\ of\ kilometers\ (EU\ only)}$$ | | Conduct trainings for better identification of transport bundles based on early order variables |
| | | | Analyze existing framework agreements and renegotiate where appropriate |
| | | | Reduction the total number of supplier to build up of market power |
| 02 Reduce handling costs | Average order costs: $$\frac{Sum\ of\ internal\ staff\ costs}{Total\ number\ of\ handled\ orders}$$ | | Process analysis and description of optimizations for task execution |
| | | | Outsource process activities (e. g. explain advantages in a mailing) |
| | Cost reduction by external service provider: $$\frac{(Average\ costs\ of\ external\ service) - (Average\ costs\ of\ insourcing\ solutions)}{Total\ number\ of\ external\ orders}$$ | | Insourcing of orders that were previously handled externally |
| | | | Advertise warehousing activities of external service providers |
| **Security, safety and environment perspective** | | | |
| 03 Increase information quality | Percentage of rejected requests: $$\frac{Number\ of\ requests\ stopped\ in\ the\ status\ 10}{Total\ number\ of\ requests}$$ | | Strictly refusal of orders according to the available checklist |
| | | | Analysis of the reasons for refusal in the last survey interval and seek solutions to prevent them in the future |
| 04 Increase information security | Violations of the privacy policy per order: $$\frac{Total\ number\ of\ registered\ violations}{Total\ number\ of\ handled\ orders}$$ | | Implement regular training for own employees regarding matters of information security |
| | | | Foster instructions and awareness in daily work routines |
| | | | Make this issue explicit on the intranet of the department (including FAQs) |
| 05 Minimization of damages | Loss rate: $$\frac{Total\ number\ of\ documented\ damages}{Total\ number\ of\ handled\ orders}$$ | | Implement an MS Access database for the documentation of all damages |
| | | | Analysis of damages occurred per service provider |
| | | | Provide proposals for the reduction of damages to service providers |

## Partner perspective

### Logistic service provider

| 06 | Increase transport quality | Complaint rate:<br>$$\frac{\text{Number of complaints regarding wrong delivery quality}}{\text{Total number of handled orders}}$$ | Consider the delivery time for all transports in the database |
|---|---|---|---|
| | | | Implementation of an e-mail survey at the end of each order |
| | | | Analysis of survey responses |
| 07 | Increase data correctness | Complaint costs:<br>$$\frac{\text{Expenditures for complaints}}{\text{Total number of handled orders}}$$ | Develop proposals for the implementation of IT-based plausibility checks for new orders |
| 08 | Make payments correctly | Proportion of wrong data:<br>$$\frac{\text{Number of orders with wrong variables leading to incorrect payments}}{\text{Total number of handled orders}}$$ | Re-weighing of a random sample and document all weight deviations (lessons learned) |
| | | | Review tooltips which explain the importance of weights in the logistics portal |
| | | | Analysis of wrong weights and incorrect payments |

### Internal customer

| 09 | Meet customer expectations | Internal rate of complaints:<br>$$\frac{\text{Number of complaints from internal customers}}{\text{Total number of handled orders}}$$ | Implement the option to submit and document complaints directly as part of an order (register card) |
|---|---|---|---|
| | | | Introduce the option to submit a complaint in the e-mail notification at the end of an order |
| | | | Expand awareness efforts by upgrading the intranet presentation (e. g. presentation of processes) |

### Process team

| 10 | Increase employee productivity | Time spent on processing:<br>$$\frac{\text{Total employee time}}{\text{Total number of handled orders}}$$ | Train employees to follow the existing process definitions |
|---|---|---|---|
| | | | Acquire new business fields (in addition to current services) |
| | | | Introduce a software tool for capturing the necessary information |
| 11 | Increase motivation | Turnover rate:<br>$$\frac{\text{Number of departures}}{\text{Average number of employees}}$$ | Organize regular JFs |
| | | | Implement feedback sessions for team leads |
| | | | Increase the number of persons participating in the development center |

### Authorities

| 12 | Meet official requirements | Number of mandatory incidents per order:<br>$$\frac{\text{Number of mandatory incidents}}{\text{Total number of transports}}$$ | Implement an obligatory registration of all transport objects (even if not required by law) |
|---|---|---|---|
| | | | Implement splitting of supplier tickets |
| | | | Up-to-date training on changes to standards and laws |
| 13 | Intensify cooperation | Degree of cooperation (internal survey):<br>$$\frac{\text{Average assessment of employees}}{\text{Maximum number of possible points}}$$ | Establish annual compliance training for all employees |
| | | | Implement customs training and moderated sharing of experiences |
| | | | Introduce a database for the documentation of frequent errors and recognize these results in the training sessions |

## Business processes and projects

| | | | |
|---|---|---|---|
| 14 | Reduction of exceptions | Exception ratio:<br><br>$$\frac{\text{Number of process instances}}{\text{that are not running according to}}$$<br>$$\frac{\text{a process definition}}{\text{Total number of process instances}}$$ | Perform analysis of exceptions (including lessons learned) |
| | | | Make visa applications available in the IT system with a suitable process definition |
| | | | Implement special training for people who frequently cause extra trips as process exceptions |
| 15 | Prevent interfaces | Integration rate:<br><br>$$\frac{\text{Number of interfaces}}{\text{that cause manual work}}$$<br>$$\frac{\text{Total number of physical}}{\text{and IT interfaces}}$$ | Bridge interface between SAP and the logistics portal (specification and implementation of a solution) |
| | | | Bridge interface between the DHL portal and the logistics portal (specification and implementation of a solution) |
| | | | Creation of new process definitions and no further usage of the SAP system XY. |
| 16 | Optimize data capturing | Rejection rate:<br><br>$$\frac{\text{Total number of valid data sets}}{\text{Total number of data sets}}$$ | Improve the checklist for the consistent refusal of orders |
| | | | Implement documentation of manual post-corrections |
| 17 | Increase process transparency | Transparency according to internal customers:<br><br>$$\frac{\text{Total number of points awarded}}{\text{for transparency}}$$<br>$$\frac{}{\text{Total number of possible points}}$$ | Increase number of process actors (e. g. internal customers), who can track the status of an instance |
| | | | Make the status of an order available in the intranet |
| | | | Specify and implement connection to the external tracing system of Schenker |

## Learning and growth

| | | | |
|---|---|---|---|
| 18 | Force the usage of IT | Proportion of IT integration:<br><br>$$\frac{\text{Number of}}{\text{integrated IT systems}}$$<br>$$\frac{}{\text{Number of possible integrations}}$$ | Design and implement additional features for the logistics portal |
| | | | Automate invoice creation |
| | | | Make shipments of class 7 available in the internal portal |
| 19 | Increase awareness for logistic services | Internal agreement rate (annual customer survey):<br><br>$$\frac{\text{Sum of the given points}}{\text{for awareness}}$$<br>$$\frac{}{\text{Maximal number of}}$$<br>$$\text{possible points}$$ | Implement training concept for new employees |
| | | | Motivate internal customers to submit recommendations for further improvements (e. g. in a mailing) |
| | | | Establish marketing actions at each customer contact |
| | | | Improve intranet presentation of the logistics processes |
| | | | Address the issue of awareness as an explicit topic on the intranet |
| 20 | Increase sphere of influence | Average agreement (annual customer survey):<br><br>$$\frac{\text{Number of respondent who agree}}{\text{that BEX} - \text{G provides good advice}}$$<br>$$\frac{}{\text{Total number of respondents}}$$ | Address the of issue of influence in the senior management committee and provide particular solutions |
| | | | Establish marketing activities at all departments |
| | | | Create intranet messages with detailed arguments on this subject |
| 21 | Intensify LSP management | Rate of managed suppliers:<br><br>$$\frac{\text{Number of suppliers which are}}{\text{fully evaluated in the system}}$$<br>$$\frac{}{\text{Total number of}}$$<br>$$\text{documented suppliers}$$ | Design and implement an IT system for LSP management |
| | | | Document and manage the current suppliers with comprehensive information in the new IT system |

# B    Scientific Development Approach

As described in the introduction of this book, the original form of the BSC often reaches its limits and implies various risks. All presented **ingredients** for a successful BSC were originally developed in a research project, which analyzed literature in order to summarize fundamental rules, called **principles**, for a successful and modern BSC. This appendix summarizes the basic research approach.

This research was able to document six generic principles for success based on a comprehensive state-of-the-art analysis of a total of 30 separate publications. All generic principles have been equipped with specific recommendations for business practice, on what constitutes a successful and modern BSC.

The term **principle** was used to indicate that no single success factor should be developed. As outlined in Figure 30, principles will develop and document rather fundamental rules and directions of impact, which can be deduced from the individual factors.

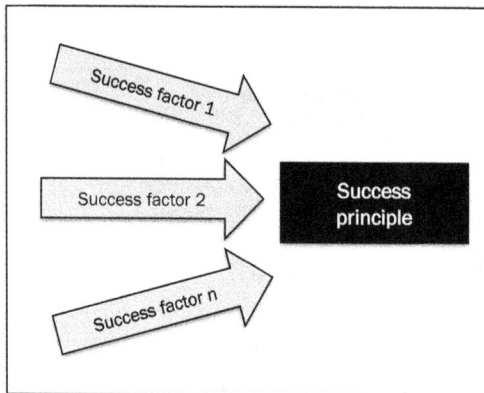

Figure 30: Connection between individual factors or derivatives and principles
[Source: own illustration]

This chapter describes what can be defined as success factors. Then the research method is outlined and systematically applied to identify the success principles, which are the fundamental base for the ingredients presented in chapter 3.

Success factor refer to all actions and general conditions of an organization that can be directly and indirectly influenced, and which are positively correlated to the success of a BSC.

## B.1  General Methodology

This research used the method of meta-analysis, in particular an integrative review approach, to deal with the formulated research tasks. According to Kornmeier (2007, pp. 137ff.) this method is especially suitable for research with the aim of providing an overview and establishing general and fundamental statements based on the information currently available (analysis of an analysis). This was very much in line with the objective to generate general success based on scientific research. In addition, this particular type of research is often used when very different sources of literature are available on the topic in question and when they need to be summarized in a contemporary form (Oermann and Hays 2010, pp. 138ff.; Hart 2006, p.19).

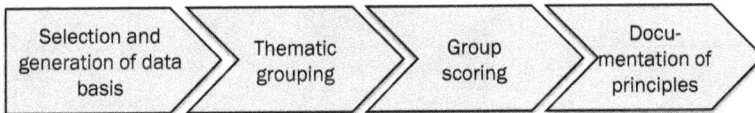

Figure 31: Methodology to derive principles for success and further development
[Source: own illustration]

In order to meet the research challenges, a generic four stage approach (as depicted in Figure 31) was applied, which was based on the integrative review methodology as described (Kornmeier 2007, pp. 137ff.; Oermann and Hays 2010, pp. 138ff.; Hart 2006, p.19):

- **Selection and generation of data base**: The first step was to establish criteria to define which data sources needed to be taken into account and which sources can or should be dismissed. Suitable sources in literature were then identified to generate the basis of the analysis.

- **Thematic grouping**: Success factors or derivatives including the same or similar statements about a certain aspect or content as well as those which might be on a different level of detail, but which are, however, related to each other by their subject were grouped together in so called **thematic groups**. Each group was summarized under a title.

- **Group scoring**: In the next step, the different thematic groups were evaluated, according to objective and verifiable standards. A score for each group indicates the relevance and importance of the respective thematic group. The groups which reached a comparatively high score (SC) were from then on be classified as principle (P) and later used as ingredient. A suitable scoring method was chosen depending on the number of groups and the type of data source.

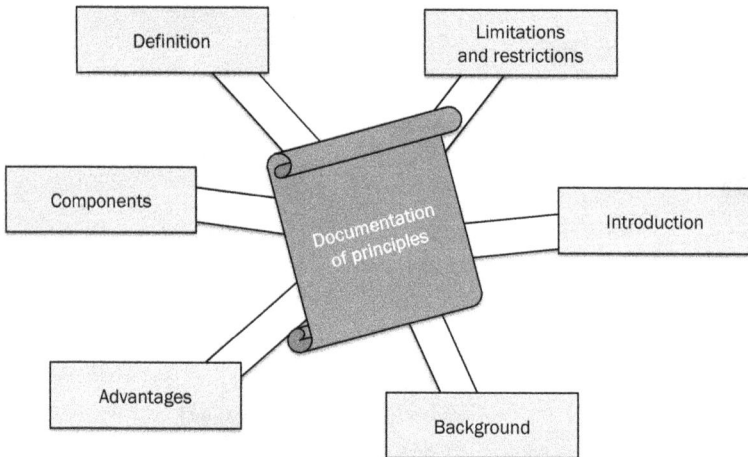

Figure 32: Documentation template for success and further development principles
[Source: own illustration adopted from Flores et al. (2009, p. 113)]

- **Documentation of principles:** As the developed principles could be seen as **best practices**[13], the template of good management practices by Flores et al. (2009, p. 113) was used for their documentation (see Figure 32):
  o **Definition:** Each principle must be clearly defined and is differentiated by a short description.
  o **Background:** To permit understanding the principle in its historical or conceptual context, principles are documented together with their background.
  o **Components:** The aim is to show which ideas and elements of the principle cooperate in order to generate added value.
  o **Advantages:** This aspect describes the benefits and reasons of certain advantages so as to establish the positive effects of the principle's application.
  o **Limitations and restrictions:** In order to be able to decide later whether an application of the principle is possible in a particular case, limitations and restrictions for the implementation of the principle are documented.
  o **Introduction:** The introduction strategy describes how to put the principle into practice.

An analysis of the literature on success factors provided the following general aspects:

- **Specific perspective:** Mostly, success factors and further developments were documented in a well-defined area (e. g. SMEs, specific industries or countries, etc.).
- **Lack of uniformity:** In part, the same success factors were mentioned in different sources, but some, however, also differed significantly from each other and were partly non-consistent.

---

[13] In this context, a "best practice" has the explicit aim to generate top performance and shows the way to success which can be transferred to other enterprises and issues (Markert et al. 2008, pp. 99ff.; Krems 2009; Gandor and Langen 2008, p. 78). Since these characteristics are also accurate for the principles of this research, it seems reasonable to use a template for the documentation of best practices.

- **Lack of analysis**: No detailed analyses were available which provided a systematic comparison of success factors. Although there were a few sources which describe an overview (e. g. Siepermann and Vockeroth 2009), these texts, however, only presented success factors in an arbitrary and unrelated manner. Thus, these sources could not claim completeness and did not offer a profound analysis.
- **Different abstraction levels**: The representations varied strongly in terms of detail. Some statements quite elaborately described very detailed success factors (setting up cost centers for the operation of a BSC, for example). Some publications, on the other hand, remained very general and generic (the unspecified call for open communication, for example).
- **Same message**: Some success factors resemble each other or are even almost identical. The actual wording of the statements was different, so that they could not be considered as linguistically equivalent, but nevertheless referred to the same content.

As an interim conclusion, it could be assumed that current research lacks analyses that consistently describe the success factors at a comparable level of abstraction or which formulate a doctrine which can generate additional value.

## B.2 Success Principles

In this chapter the methodological approach as outlined is applied to establish success principles. The reference details of the sources from literature, the initial thematic groups and the applied scoring can be found in Table 3.

Table 3: Meta analysis

| Literature reference | | Literature content | | Comment | Thematic groups | | | | | | |
|---|---|---|---|---|---|---|---|---|---|---|---|
| ID | Source | T | F | Background of source | G1 | G2 | G3 | G4 | G5 | G6 | G7 |
| 1 | Bodmer and Völker 2000 | T | 6 | Benchmarking of five users | S | P | S | S | P | S | N |
| 2 | Hendricks, Menor and Wiedmann 2004 | T | 8 | Empirical study | N | S | P | S | P | S | N |
| 3 | Lawson, Stratton and Hatch 2006 | T | 5 | Survey of practitioners | P | P | P | N | P | N | N |
| 4 | McCunn 1998 | T | 10 | Study of seven users; negative wording | P | S | P | N | S | S | N |
| 5 | Morisawa and Kurosaki 2003 | T | 6 | Empirical study for Japan | S | N | P | N | P | P | N |
| 6 | Olve et al. 2004 | T | 6 | Based on case study analysis | N | P | S | S | P | N | N |
| 7 | Othman et al. 2006 | T | 7 | Analysis in Malaysia; negative wording | S | P | S | S | N | P | N |
| 8 | Peters 2008 | T | 7 | Theoretical deduction from original concept | N | S | P | P | S | N | N |
| 9 | Richardson 2004 | T | 6 | Study on different experiences | N | N | P | N | P | S | N |
| 10 | Ringe 2006 | T | 7 | Theoretical deduction from original concept | N | N | S | P | S | S | P |
| 11 | Crespo et al. 2009 | E | 9 | Guidelines for SMEs | P | N | S | S | P | S | S |
| 12 | Ghosh and Mukherjee 2006 | E | 8 | Introduction to BSC | N | S | S | P | N | S | N |
| 13 | Hyperspace 2010 | E | 19 | Report by a consulting firm; negative wording | S | S | S | S | P | P | S |
| 14 | Mair 2002 | E | 5 | Guidelines for practice; negative wording | P | N | N | P | P | S | N |
| 15 | Niven 2002 | E | 10 | Complete textbook on BSC; negative wording | S | S | S | S | P | S | N |
| 16 | PricewaterhouseCoopers n.d. | E | 6 | Presentation by a consulting company | P | N | N | N | P | N | N |
| 17 | Schmeisser and Clausen 2009 | E | 9 | Textbook on BSC | P | S | N | S | P | S | N |
| 18 | Value Competence Consulting 2002 | E | 5 | Introductory presentation; negative wording | P | N | N | P | P | P | N |
| 19 | Vohl 2004 | E | 8 | Controlling guidelines for SMEs | P | S | S | S | P | N | S |
| 20 | Weber and Schäffer 2000 | E | 7 | Report of experiences in education | P | N | N | N | P | N | N |
| 21 | Angel and Rampersad 2005 | P | 10 | Experiences of a consultant | S | S | S | S | P | S | N |
| 22 | Bauer 2010 | P | 10 | Experiences of one single company | P | P | S | N | S | S | N |
| 23 | Blackall 2007 | P | 5 | Experiences of a consultant | P | N | P | N | P | N | N |
| 24 | Harber 1998 | P | 5 | Experiences in a special branch | N | N | N | P | P | P | P |
| 25 | Kaplan and Norton 1996 | P | 4 | Barriers documented by the authors | N | P | P | N | P | N | S |
| 26 | Kaplan and Norton 2001 | P | 5 | Experience of strategy implementation | N | P | P | N | P | P | S |
| 27 | Niven 1998 | P | 7 | Examination of one business case | S | P | S | N | S | S | P |
| 28 | Pandey 2005 | P | 8 | Experiences in USA and India | N | P | P | S | P | N | N |
| 29 | Schermann and Volcic 2009 | P | 10 | Generic experiences based on one sector | N | S | S | S | N | N | N |
| 30 | Williams 2004 | P | 6 | Report of a specialized consulting firm | S | S | S | S | S | S | N |
| Number of factors | | | 224 | Score of thematic group | 41 | 40 | 44 | 31 | 69 | 32 | 14 |

**Legend**

| Literature reference and literature content | Thematic groups | |
|---|---|---|
| ID: Identification number | G1 | Planning and introduction |
| T: Type | G2 | Integration |
| F: Number of factors | G3 | Cascading |
| E: Educational texts | G4 | Measurement |
| P: Statements of experts and practitioners | G4 | Acceptance and support |
| T: Theories and studies | G6 | Continuous process |
| | G7 | Rule-following |
| | **Evaluation** | |
| | N | None |
| | S | Significant |
| | P | Primary |

[Source: own illustration]

## Selection and Generation of Data Basis

This analysis was based on three types of literature that were each weighted equally, i. e. with one third of importance, in order to provide a balanced data base:

- **Educational texts (E):** Even if usually textbooks and manuals are not adequate as scientific sources (De Bie and Kool 2004, pp. 141ff.), there is still a reason why they should be taken into account in this project. Educational texts usually present a simplified and introductory view (Ebster and Stalzer 2003, p.

259). For this particular piece of research, of course this type of source cannot be used alone, but the explicit aim of this analysis is to formulate best practices, allowing the instructions gained to be transferred to other areas and companies later on. Therefore, considering educational texts as simplified and basic representations seemed permissible and even necessary for the purpose of transfer.

- **Statements of experts and practitioners (P)**: The opinions of experienced practitioners are to be seen as one important type of knowledge. One major requirement for classifying such data sources as relevant was that evidence of the author's experience is given in the text.
- **Theories and studies (T)**: In contrast to the statements of experts and practitioners, theories and studies do not reflect a personal opinion but are the result of observations or evaluations from an external position, and based on objective methods (e. g. empirical or logical deduction). This type of establishment of data was necessary to recognize implicit conditions, which were perhaps not documented explicitly in expert reports and educational texts.

This research also explicitly included sources that state negative formulations (pitfalls for BSCs, for example), as long as they could be accurately translated into corresponding success factors (the pitfall of ignoring the connection of all initiatives to vision and strategy, for example, could be translated into the call for linking all initiatives to vision and strategy).

### Thematic Grouping

Some individual factors referred to the same content, but were worded differently (some sources, for example, recommend the use of standard software to support the BSC concept, while others suggest overall IT support of the BSC). These statements were pooled.

To classify real principles thematically, similar statements as well as similar pools were condensed into thematic groups (the integration of IT support can be seen as a general interaction with structures given in a company; this integration may also include incentive systems, process frameworks and other concepts).

From the analyses seven thematic groups emerge (see later in Figure 33, p. 148).

### Group Scoring

In the previous step, 224 individual factors from 30 sources in literature were examined to generate the groups. So as to measure group relevance, a number scoring model was applied, which was based on a three-point scale:

- **Significant (s):** If a success factor which could be associated with a thematic group was mentioned in a source of literature at least once, this source was considered as **significant** for supporting the thematic group (a, number of significant nominations per thematic group).
- **Primary (p):** If several factors in one source of literature could be associated to a thematic group and if their percentage in the source exceeded 25%, this source was considered to be a **primary** source (b, number of primary nominations per thematic group), supporting the thematic group (according to the number of primary nominations per thematic group).
- **None (n):** If a factor was not mentioned in the particular source, it was not to be considered in the scoring (**none**).

The individual components were each weighted according to the frequency at which they were mentioned. Significant statements (s) were accorded with the factor one. Since primary statements were clearly weighted with a higher factor in scientific literature, they received the factor of three. The relevance of a thematic group was defined using the following formula, which summed up the total group score ($SC_{group}$):

$$SC_{group} = \sum_{\alpha=1}^{a} s_\alpha + \sum_{\beta=1}^{b} p_\beta \cdot 3$$

After each group has then received a score, the following formula was used to determine which thematic group had a particularly high relevance and should therefore be classified as a principle:

$$SC_{group} > \frac{SC_{max}}{3}$$

Of all the thematic groups, those were determined as principles which were at least named once as primary (p). With 30 sources taken into account, the maximum score achievable ($SC_{max}$) was 90 and a scoring threshold of 30 was necessary for the classification as principle.

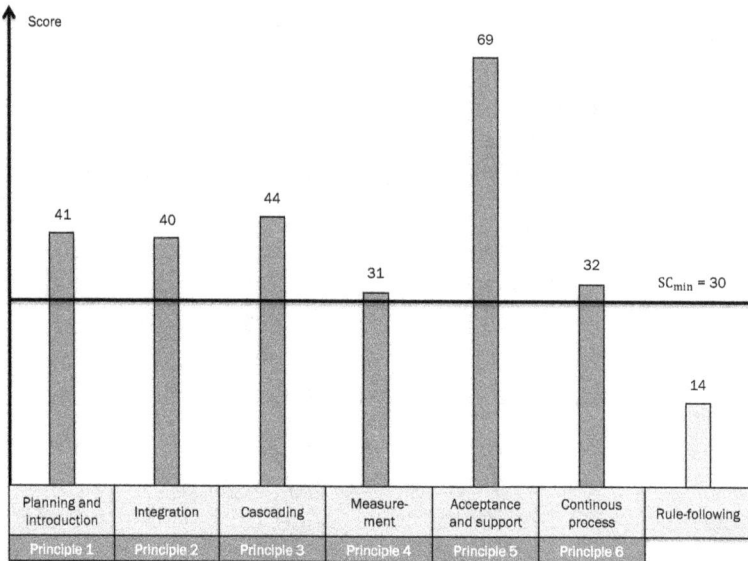

Figure 33: Scoring of thematic groups
[Source: own illustration]

Figure 33 shows the score (SC) of the seven thematic groups.

### Documentation of Principles

From the original seven thematic groups, only six groups[14] met the requirement of a score higher than 30, as defined above, and were therefore considered as principles (P)[15]. Figure 34 outlines the success principles.

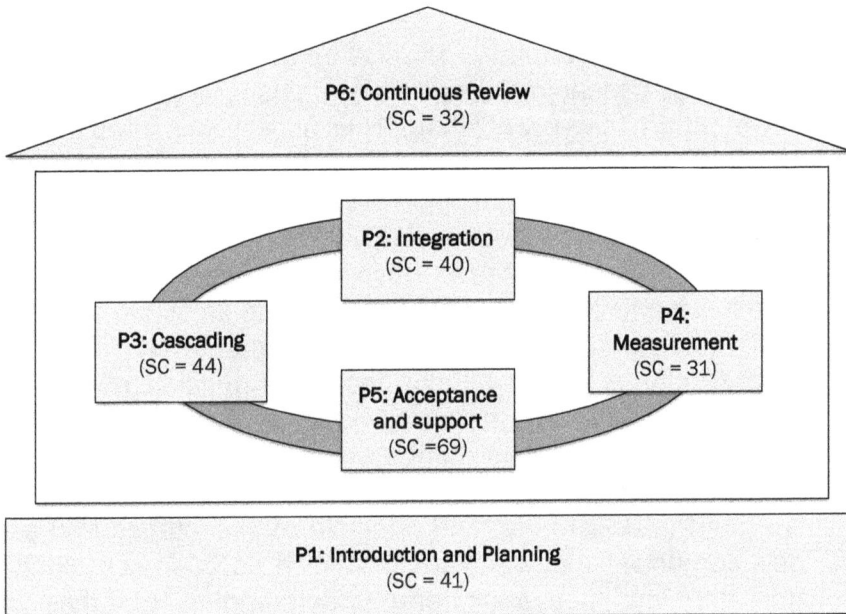

Figure 34: Success principles of the BSC with corresponding score
[Source: own illustration]

The fundamental success principles of the BSC according to the meta-analysis are:

- **Planning and introduction**: This principle describes that the project management, implementation strategy and the plan-

---

[14] The group "rule-following" sums up the statements that call for a precise and unconditional compliance with the rules of the BSC as well as with its architecture (design of perspectives, for example). This thematic group did not have a sufficient relevance (SCgroup 7 = 14).

[15] From now on, the capital letter "P" stands for "principle".

ning of a BSC project all have an important impact on the overall success of the BSC. The principle calls for pilot studies and for external consultants as well as for the usage of a best-practice implementation process.

- **Integration:** The BSC must be adapted very closely to the current configuration of an organization. Taking into account different frameworks and systems (process frameworks, incentive systems, IT support, risk management, and allocation processes, for example) is decisive for the BSC success.

- **Cascading:** Cascading describes a meaningful strategy breakdown within the organization. This aspect is particularly important for the functioning of a BSC. Components of this principle are the question of finding a suitable level of detail, an approach for the break-down of BSCs into individual steps and the support of employees at the lowest cascading level.

- **Measurement:** Many sources describe the selection, balance, designation and communication of measures and targets as an essential as well as difficult task. This principle documents compulsory as well as balanced aspects which are necessary for a successful measurement system.

- **Acceptance and support:** It is up to the employees to ultimately bring the BSC to life. The principle of acceptance and support comprises many soft factors, such as open communication, training, motivation, and understanding, and has the highest principle score. Moreover, this principle recommends specific actions that make employees of a particular organization accept and support the BSC approach.

- **Continuous process:** It does not seem to be sufficient to create a balanced score card once, but it seems highly important to implement a continuous process. Due to changes in the business environment (technological developments, for example) and also due to internal changes (like alterations in the company vision), the BSC continually has to be reviewed and improved.

A detailed and full documentation of these general success principles with all factors of the description scheme can be found in the ingredients of chapter 3.

# References

**Angel and Rampersad 2005**

Angel, Robert; Rampersad, Hubert (2005): Do Scorecards Add Up. In: CA-magazine 138 (4), pp. 30-35.

**Barthélemy et al. 2010**

Barthélemy, Frank; Knöll, Heinz-Dieter; Salfeld, André; Schulz-Sacharow, Christoph; Vögele, Dorothee (2010): Balanced Scorecard: Erfolgreiche IT-Auswahl, Einführung und Anwendung: Unternehmen berichten. Viewig und Teubner, Wiesbaden.

**Bauer 2010**

Bauer, Georg (2010): Strategisches Management in einer Autobank mit der Balanced Scorecard. In: Stenner, F. (Ed.): Handbuch Automobilbanken: Finanzdienstleistungen für Mobilität. Springer, Heidelberg, pp. 275-285.

**Bible, Kerr and Zanini 2006**

Bible, Lynn; Kerr, Stephen; Zanini, Michael (2006): The Balanced Scorecard: Here and Back. In: Management Accounting Quarterly 7 (4), pp. 18-23.

**Blackall 2007**

Blackall, Gren (2007): How to Implement a Balanced Scorecard. In: Maine Community Banker 2, pp. 8-9.

**Bodmer and Völker 2000**

Bodmer, Christian; Völker, Rainer (2000): Erfolgsfaktoren bei der Implementierung einer Balanced Scorecard. In: Controlling 12 (10), pp. 477-484.

**Brain & Company 2011**

Brain & Company (2011): Management Tools & Trends 2011.

**Broccardo 2010**

Broccardo, Laura (2010): An empirical study of the Balanced Scorecard as a flexible strategic management and reporting tool. In: Economia Aziendale Online 2000 Web 4 (2), pp. 81-91.

### Chandler 1969

Chandler, Alfred D. (1969): Strategy and Structure: Chapters in the History of the American Industrial Enterprise. In: MIT Press 22.

### Crespo et al. 2009

Crespo, Isabel; Bergmann, Lars; Portmann, Stefan; Lacker, Thomas; Lacker, Michael; Fleischmann, Jürgen; Kozó, Hans (2009): Umsetzung der Unternehmensstrategie mit der Balanced Scorecard. In: Dombrowski, U.; Herrmann, C.; Lacker, T.; Sonnentag, S. (Eds.): Modernisierung kleiner und mittlerer Unternehmen: Ein ganzheitliches Konzept. Springer, Heidelberg, pp. 136-150.

### Cross and Lynch 1998

Cross, Kelvin F.; Lynch, Richard L. (1998): Measure Up! How to Measure Corporate Performance. Cambridge, Oxford.

### De Bie and Kool 2004

De Bie, Rob; Kool, Jan (2004): Wissenschaftliches Arbeiten. In: Hüter-Becker, A. (Ed.): Beruf, Recht, wissenschaftliches Arbeiten. Thieme, Stuttgart, pp. 130-230.

### Dressler 2004

Dressler, Soeren (2004): Strategy, Organizational Effectiveness and Performance Management - From Basics to Best Practices. Universal, Florida.

### Ebster and Stalzer 2003

Ebster, Claus; Stalzer, Lieselotte (2003): Wissenschaftliches Arbeiten für Wirtschafts- und Sozialwissenschaftler. Facultas, Wien.

### Edinger 2009

Edinger, Jochen (2009): Führen mit organisationalen Zielen - Erfahrungen im öffentlichen Dienstleistungsbereich. In: Schwaab, O.; Bergmann, G.; Gairing, F.; Kolb, M. (Eds.): Führen mit Zielen: Konzepte - Erfahrungen - Erfolgsfaktoren. Gabler, Wiesbaden, pp. 226-249.

### Eicker, Kress and Lelke 2005

Eicker, Stefan; Kress, Stephan; Lelke, Frank (2005): Kennzahlengestützte Geschäftssteuerung im Dienstleistungssektor - Ergebnisse einer empirischen Untersuchung. In: Zeitschrift für Controlling & Management 6, pp. 408-414.

**Eilers 2005**

Eilers, Nadja (2005): Balanced Scorecard als Instrument der internen Steuerung und des externen Reporting. Seminar Thesis, Institut für Wirtschaftsprüfung und Steuerwesen, Universität Hamburg.

**Engel 2006**

Engel, Andreas (2006): Wertschöpfungsorientierte Balanced Scorecard: Entwicklung und Ausgestaltung eines strategieumsetzungsorientierten Ziel- und Kennzahlensystems. Kovač, Hamburg.

**Fahey and Narayanan 1986**

Fahey, Liam; Narayanan, Vijaykrishnan K. (1986): Macroenvironmental Analysis for Strategic Management. St. Paul, Minnesota.

**FAZ 2005**

FAZ (2005): Chrysler hat in China großes Potential - Rüdiger Grube im Interview.

**Flores et al. 2009**

Flores, Myrna; Mendoza, Ana; Lavin, Victor; Flores, Benito (2009): Developing a Taxonomy and Model to Transfer and Assess Best Practices for SCM. In: Leveraging Knowledge for Innovation in Collaborative Networks - 10th IFIP 5 (5), pp. 7-9.

**Frigo and Krumwiede 1999**

Frigo, Mark L.; Krumwiede, Kip R. (1999): Balanced Scorecards - A Rising Trend in Strategic Performance Measurement. In: Journal of Strategic Performance Measurement 3 (1), pp. 42-48.

**Gaiser and Greiner 2002**

Gaiser, Bernd; Greiner, Oliver (2002): Strategische Steuerung: Von der Balanced Scorecard zur strategie-fokussierten Organisation. In: Gleich, R.; Möller, K.; Seidenschwarz, W.; Stoi, R. (Eds.): Controllingfortschritte. Vahlen, München, pp. 193-222.

**Gandor and Langen 2008**

Gandor, Corinna; Langen, Rainer (2008): Quo vadis, Kita?. Book-on-demand.de, Norderstedt.

**Ghosh and Mukherjee 2006**

Ghosh, Samir; Mukherjee, Subrata (2006): Measurement of corporate performance through Balanced Scorecard: An overview. In: Vidyasagar University Journal of Commerce, 11-2006 (3), pp. 60-70.

**Girmscheid 2006**

Girmscheid, Gerhard (2006): Strategisches Bauunternehmensmanagement: prozessorientiertes integriertes Management für Unternehmen in der Bauwirtschaft. Springer, Berlin.

**Gladen 2003**

Gladen, Werner (2003): Kennzahlen- und Berichtssysteme - Grundlagen zum Performance Measurement. Gabler, Wiesbaden.

**Gleich 2001**

Gleich, Ronald (2001): Das System des Performance Measurements. Vahlen, München.

**Haid 2003**

Haid, Dirk (2003): Corporate Entrepreneurship im strategischen Management: Ansatz zur Implementierung des Unternehmertums im Unternehmen. DUV, Wiesbaden.

**Harber 1998**

Harber, Bruce W. (1998): The Balanced Scorecard - Solution at Peel Memorial Hospital. In: Healthcare Quarterly 1 (4), pp. 59-63.

**Hart 2006**

Hart, Chris (2006): Doing a literature review - releasing the social science research imagination. Sage, London.

**Haunerdinger and Probst 2006**

Haunerdinger, Monika; Probst, Hans-Jürgen (2006): BWL visuell: Basiswissen für Fortbildung und Praxis. Cornelsen, Berlin.

**Hendricks, Menor and Wiedmann 2004**

Hendricks, Kevin; Menor, Larry; Wiedman, Christine (2004): The Balanced Scorecard: To Adopt or Not to Adopt?. In: Ivey Business Journal 69 (2), pp. 1-6.

**Hoffmann 1999**

Hoffmann, Olaf (1999): Performance Management Systeme und Implementierungsansätze. Haupt, Bern.

**Horvath & Partners 2004**

Horvath & Partners (2004): Balanced Scorecard umsetzen. Schäffer-Poeschel, Stuttgart.

**Horvath & Partners 2007**

Horvath & Partners (2007): Balanced Scorecard umsetzen. Schäffer-Poeschel, Stuttgart.

**Horvath and Kaufmann 1998**

Horvath, Peter; Kaufmann, Lutz (1998): Balanced Scorecard - ein Werkzeug zur Umsetzung von Strategien. In: Harvard Businessmanager 20 (5), pp. 39-48.

**Hyperspace 2010**

Hyperspace (2010): Einführung in die Balanced Scorecard - Konzept, Methodik und Implementierung im Unternehmen.

**Kaplan and Norton 1992**

Kaplan, Robert S.; Norton, David P. (1992): The Balanced Scorecard - Measures that Drive Performance. In: Harvard Business Review 1992 January/February, pp. 71-79.

**Kaplan and Norton 1996**

Kaplan, Robert S.; Norton, David P. (1996): Using the balanced scorecard as a strategic management system. Harvard Business Review 1992 January/February, pp. 75-85.

**Kaplan and Norton 1997**

Kaplan, Robert S.; Norton, David P. (1997): Balanced Scorecard – Strategien erfolgreich umsetzen. Schäffer-Poeschel, Stuttgart.

**Kaplan and Norton 2001**

Kaplan, Robert S.; Norton, David P. (1997): Die strategiefokussierte Organisation – Führen mit der Balanced Scorecard. Schäffer-Poeschel, Stuttgart.

**Kaplan and Norton 2001b**

Kaplan, Robert S.; Norton, David P. (2001): Transforming the Balanced Scorecard from performance measurement to strategic management - Part 1. In: Accounting Horizons 15 (1), pp. 87-104.

### König and Rehling 2002

König, Susanne; Rehling, Mette (2001): Zur Übertragbarkeit der Balanced Scorecard auf ein zukunftsgerichtetes Personalmanagement der öffentlichen Verwaltung. Universität Oldenburg PerMit Diskussionspapier, Oldenburg.

### Kornmeier 2007

Kornmeier, Martin (2007): Wissenschaftstheorie und wissenschaftliches Arbeiten: Eine Einführung für Wirtschaftswissenschaftler. Physica, Mannheim.

### Krause 2006

Krause, Oliver (2006): Performance Management: Eine Stakeholder-Nutzen-orientierte und Geschäftsprozess-basierte Methode. DUV, Berlin.

### Krems 2009

Krems, Burkhardt (2009): Best Practice.

### Lauzel and Cibert 1959

Lauzel, Pierre; Cibert, André (1959): Des ratios au tableau de bord - From ratios to management reporting. Entreprise moderne d'edition, Paris.

### Lawson, Stratton and Hatch 2006

Lawson, Raef A.; Stratton, William G.; Hatch, Toby (2005): Scorecarding in Northern Amercia: Moving towards a Best-Practices Framework, Part 1. In: Journal of Cost Management Juli/August, pp. 25-34.

### Letza 1996

Letza, Stephen R. (1996): The design and implementation of the Balanced Business Scorecard: An analysis of three companies in practice. In: Business Process Management Journal 2 (3), pp. 54-76.

### Mair 2002

Mair, Steven (2002): A Balanced Scorecard for a Small Software Group. In: IEEE Software 19 (6), pp. 21-27.

### Markert et al. 2008

Markert, Andreas; Buckley, Andrea; Vilain, Michael; Biebricher, Martin (2008): Soziale Arbeit und Sozialwirtschaft: Beiträge zu einem Feld im Umbruch - Festschrift für Karl-Heinz Boeßenecker. LIT, Münster.

**Matlachowsky 2008**

Matlachowsky, Philip (2008): Implementierungsstand der Balanced Scorecard: Eine fallstudienbasierte Analyse der Entwicklung von Balanced Scorecards in deutschen Unternehmen. Gabler, Wiesbaden.

**McCunn 1998**

McCunn, Paul (1998): The Balanced Scorecard: The Eleventh Commandment. In: Management Accounting 76 (11), pp. 34-36.

**Meyer 2007**

Meyer, Eric (2007): CSS - Das umfassende Handbuch. O'Reilly, n.p.

**Morisawa and Kurosaki 2003**

Morisawa, Toru; Kurosaki, Hiroshi (2003): Using the Balanced Scorecard in Reforming Corporate Management Systems. In: NRI Papers 71 (1), pp. 1-14.

**Müller 2000**

Müller, Armin (2000): Strategisches Management mit der Balanced Scorecard. Kohlhammer, Stuttgart.

**Neely and Adams 2002**

Neely, Andy; Adams, Chris (2002): The Performance Prism.

**Niven 1998**

Niven, Paul R. (1998): Cascading the Balanced Scorecard.

**Niven 2002**

Niven, Paul R. (2002): Balanced Scorecard Step by Step- Maximizing Performance and Maintaining Results. John Wiley & Sons, New York.

**Niven 2009**

Niven, Paul R. (2009): Balanced Scorecard - Arbeitsbuch. Wiley, New Jersey.

**Oermann and Hays 2010**

Oermann, Marilyn H.; Hays, Judith C. (2010): Writing for Publication in Nursing. Springer, New York.

**Olve et al. 2004**

Olve, Nils-Göran; Petri, Carl-Johan; Roy, Jan; Roy, Sofie (2004): Twelve years later: understanding and realizing the value of Balanced Scorecards. In: Ivey Business Journal 685 (5), pp. 1-7.

**Othman et al. 2006**

Othman, Rozhan; Domil, Ahmad Khairy Ahmad; Senik, Zizah Che; Abdullah, Nor Liza; Hamzah, Noradiva (2006): A Case Study of Balanced Scorecard Implementation in a Malaysian Company. In: Journal of Asia-Pacific Business 7 (2), pp. 55-72.

**Pandey 2005**

Pandey, Indra Mani (2005): Balanced Scorecard: Myth and Reality. In: Vikalpa 30 (1), pp. 51-66.

**Paranjape, Rossiter and Pantano 2006**

Paranjape, Bhagyashree; Rossiter, Margaret; Pantano, Victor (2006): Insights from the Balanced Scorecard Performance measurement systems: successes, failures and future – a review. In: Measuring Business Excellence 10 (3), pp. 4-14.

**Peters 2008**

Peters, Dana (2008): Einsatz der Balanced Scorecard im Risikomanagement. Salzwasser, Paderborn.

**Pfaff 2004**

Pfaff, Dietmar (2004): Praxishandbuch Marketing - Grundlagen und Instrumente. Campus, Frankfurt am Main.

**Preißner 2007**

Preißner, Andreas (2007): Balanced Scorecard anwenden - kennzahlengestützte Unternehmenssteuerung. Hanser, München.

**Preuss 2002**

Preuss, Peter (2002): IT-gestützte Balanced Scorecard-Systeme. DUV, Mannheim.

**PricewaterhouseCoopers 2001**

PricewaterhouseCoopers (2001): Die Balanced Scorecard im Praxistest: Wie zufrieden sind Anwender?

**PricewaterhouseCoopers n.d.**

PricewaterhouseCoopers (n.d.): Balanced Scorecard – Grundzüge und Erfahrungen.

**Reichert 2006**

Reichert, Jürgen (2006): Performance Measurement in Supply Chains: Balanced Scorecard in Wertschöpfungsnetzwerken. Gabler, Wiesbaden.

**Richardson 2004**

Richardson, Sandy (2004): The Key Elements of Balanced Scorecard Success. In: Ivey Business Journal 69 (2), pp. 7-9.

**Rigby 2003**

Rigby, Darrell (2003): Management Tools Survey 2003: Usage Up As Companies Strive to Make Headway in Tough Times. In: Strategy & Leadership 31 (5), pp. 4-11.

**Ringe 2006**

Ringe, Sabine (2006): Performance Improvement Management und Balanced Scorecard – Vergleich und Bewertung anhand ausgewählter Theorien. Shaker, Aachen.

**Schermann and Volcic 2009**

Schermann, Michael P.; Volcic, Klaus (2009): Die 12 Erfolgsfaktoren der Balanced Scorecard in Krankenanstalten. Grin, Norderstedt.

**Schlögl 2003**

Schlögl, Gerhard (2003): Integrierte Unternehmenskommunikation: vom einzelnen Werbemittel zur vernetzten Kommunikation. Facultas, Wien.

**Schmeisser and Clausen 2009**

Schmeisser, Wilhelm; Clausen, Lydia (2009): Controlling und Berliner Balanced Scorecard Ansatz. Oldenbourg, München.

**Schmeisser, Clausen and Schindler 2008**

Schmeisser, Wilhelm; Clausen, Lydia; Schindler, Falko (2008): Innovationsmarketingerfolgsrechnungen im Rahmen des Berliner Balanced Scorecard Ansatzes aus der Sicht einer finanzorientierten Kundenwertanalyse. In: Schmeisser, W.; Mohnkopf, H.; Hartmann, M.; Metze, G. (Eds.): Innovationserfolgsrechung - Innovationsmanagement und Schutzrechtsbewertung, Technologieportfolio, Target-Costing, Investitionskalküle und Bilanzierung von FuE-Aktivitäten. Springer, Berlin, pp. 427-471.

**Schütte, Kenning and Peters 2003**

Schütte, Reinhard; Kenning, Peter; Peters, Malte L. (2003): Entfaltung des Untersuchungsbereichs: Wissen, Beziehungen und deren Bewertung. In: Ahlert, D.; Zelewski, S. (Eds.): Motivationseffizienz in wissensintensiven Dienstleistungsnetzwerken. Institut für Produktion und Industrielles Informationsmanagement/Institut für Handelsmanagement und Netzwerkmarketing, Essen/Münster.

### Siepermann and Vockeroth 2009

Siepermann, Christoph; Vockeroth, Jan (2009): Empfehlungen zur Gestaltung einer Risiko-Balanced Scorecard für die Beschaffung. In: Bogaschewsky, R.; Eßig, M.; Lasch, R. (Eds.): Supply Management Research: Aktuelle Forschungsergebnisse 2008, Gabler, Wiesbaden, pp. 69-102.

### Sim and Koh 2001

Sim, Khim Ling; Koh, Hian Chye (2001): Balanced Scorecard: a rising Trend in Strategic Performance Measurement. In: Measuring Business Excellence 5 (2), pp. 18-27.

### Speckbacher, Bischof and Pfeiffer 2003

Speckbacher, Gerhard; Bischof, Jürgen; Pfeiffer, Thomas (2003): A Descriptive Analysis on the Implementation of Balanced Scorecards in German-speaking countries. In: Management Accounting Research 14, pp. 361-387.

### Sushil 2008

Sushil, Prasad K. (2008): How Balanced is Balanced Scorecard?. In: Global Journal of Flexible Systems Management 9 (2), pp. III - IV.

### Umbeck, Lederer and Nitze 2009

Umbeck, Tobias; Lederer, Andreas; Nitze, Joachim (2009): Strategieklärung und Controlling einer Produktionstochter in Ungarn mit Hilfe der Balanced Scorecard - Erfahrungen eines kleinen Mittelständlers. In: Kinkel, S. (Ed.): Erfolgsfaktor Standortplanung - In- und ausländische Standorte richtig bewerten. Springer, Berlin, pp. 383-399.

### Value Competence Consulting 2002

Value Competence Consulting (2002): Balanced Scorecard - Konzept, Implementierung und Anwendungsbeispiel.

### Varma and Deshmukh 2009

Varma, Siddharth; Deshmukh, S. G. (2009): Evaluating petroleum supply chain performance - Overcoming shortcomings of Balanced Scorecard. In: Global Journal of Flexible Systems Management, 10 (4), pp. 11-22.

### Schunk, Bahl and Unrau 2002

Schunk, N.; Bahl, A.; Unrau, U. (2002): Faserverstärker und Faserlaser. In: Voges, E.; Petermann, K. (Eds.): Optische Kommunikationstechnik. Springer, Berlin, pp. 719-783.

**Vohl 2004**

Vohl, Hans-Jörg (2004): Balanced Scorecard im Mittelstand. Murmann, Hamburg.

**Weber and Schäffer 2000**

Weber, Jürgen; Schäffer, Utz (2000): Balanced Scorecard & Controlling: Implementierung - Nutzen für Manager und Controller - Erfahrungen in deutschen Unternehmen. Gabler, Wiesbaden.

**Wickel-Kirsch 2001**

Wickel-Kirsch, Silke (2001): Balanced Scorecard als Instrument des Personalcontrolling. In: Clermont, A.; Schmeisser, W.; Krimphove, D. (Eds.): Strategisches Personalmanagement in globalen Unternehmen. Vahlen, München, pp. 273-289.

**Williams 2004**

Williams, Kathy (2004): What Constitutes a Successful Balanced Scorecard?. In: Strategic Finance 86 (5), pp. 19-25.

**Winkler 2002**

Winkler, Wolfgang (2002): Brennstoffzellenanlagen. Springer, Berlin.

**Wunder 2001**

Wunder, Thomas (2001): Wie konkret muss eine Balanced Scorecard sein?. In: Controller Magazin 2 (26), pp. 133-139.

**Zell 2008**

Zell, Helmut (2008): Projektmanagement. Books on Demand, Norderstedt.

## Author Biographies

**Matthias Lederer** is a research assistant and PhD student at the chair Information Systems II of the Friedrich-Alexander University of Erlangen-Nuremberg. He leads the *Business Process Transparency Management* (BPTM) research project which has the mission to align business processes and strategies in a holistic way which covers *all* dimensions of the balanced score card. Specifically, the project develops methods to devise, implement, and measure such holistic strategies. Matthias holds an MSc in International Information Systems. Before joining the chair as a research assistant, he worked at software, consulting, and industry companies as a trainee and intern.

**Dr.-Ing. Dieter Raake** has been working in the power and energy industry for more than 23 years. He started his professional career path as a test and development engineer in Siemens AG Power Generations thermo-fluid dynamic laboratories and in the gas turbine test field. Moving out of this position into development and quality related strategic tasks he got in touch with business improvement tasks and methods like Six Sigma. As director of the Business Excellence organization he was responsible for the deployment of the Six Sigma program in Siemens Power Generation and he was leading a team of MBBs, responsible for strategic project selection, coaching and mentoring of a huge number of Six Sigma projects in various locations in Europe and Asia. After several years back in the operative business as responsible Quality and Environment Manager for Power Generations Product Business Unit - he was responsible for the set-up and controlling of the business units reporting and scorecard system. In 2010 he moved to AREVA GmbH as Vice President Safety, Quality and Industrial Performance. He is leading business improvement projects and working on balanced score cards-, reporting- and visual performance managements systems and tools. He is a certified Black Belt and Master Black Belt and holds a PhD in Engineering.

**Dr. Matthias Kurz** is an IT architect at QUA-LiS NRW, a think tank of the school administration of North Rhine-Westphalia. Furthermore, he is a long-time lecturer at the Friedrich-Alexander University of Erlangen-Nuremberg. He publishes research papers on business process management, adaptive case management and the connection between strategy design and strategy implementations at several international conferences. Before joining the public service, he was a cloud architect at DATEV eG and the head of the BPM research group at the chair Information Systems II of the Friedrich-Alexander University of Erlangen-Nuremberg.